STORY POWER

TALKING WITH TEENS IN TURBULENT TIMES

STORY POWER

TALKING WITH TEENS IN TURBULENT TIMES

JOHN W. ALSTON III

with Brenda Lane Richardson

LONGMEADOW PRESS

Published by Longmeadow Press, 201 High Ridge Road, Stamford,
CT 06904. No part of this book may be reproduced or used in any
form or by any means, electronic or mechanical, including photo-
copying, recording, or by any information storage and retrieval
system, without permission in writing from the publisher.

Jacket design by Dorothy Wachtenheim

Interior design by Richard Oriolo

ISBN: 0-681-41110-4

Library of Congress Cataloging-in-Publication Data Available
Catalog Card No.: 91-21071

Printed in the United States of America

0 9 8 7 6 5 4 3 2 1

Please note that while the stories in this book are true, in many instances, the names of the people involved, as well as certain biographical details, have been changed to protect the privacy of the individuals.

To Karen and Lindsay

ACKNOWLEDGMENTS

A special thanks goes to all who have enabled this to come together. There would not be a book called *Story Power* without the dedicated, persistent and able writing assistance of Brenda Lane Richardson. Brenda interviewed me, followed me around, and pressured me under the tightest schedule I've ever had. Throughout this collaborative endeavor, she bounced ideas and concepts up and down and around and through, forcing me to do what I had to do as we wrote, talked and gave birth to the manuscript.

To Adrienne Ingrum of Longmeadow Press, who said yes to the idea of "Story Power." To my agent, Micky Fisher, a godsend, and Jane Schafer. To Gail Larsen, who said, "Hey, you've got a book," and all but ironed me out flat from Phoenix to Honolulu, so as to level every wrinkle.

For helping me to grow in ways I thought unimaginable, Dennis Prager and his wife Fran. For taking time to help, Murry Schiller, John Mary and JaiHonna German, who had their own stories about growing up and raising teenagers. For their research assistance, Dr. Lorraine Bonner, Nancy McDonald, Barry Shapiro and Sandy Ferguson of Legworks. And, Dr. Susan Jeffers who gave inspiration from the heart.

To all of my mentors and teachers: Bob Mager, Dr. Glen Toney, Byron Kunisawa, Pat Hurley, Mark Scharonbroich, Dan Clark, Roger Crawford, June Thompson, Norm Hull, Steve Southered and Patricia Fripp. To my best friend and brother, Afriye Quamina, who modeled love and commitment, and to Doug Yeaman, who articulated its fundamentals, inspiring me to "just do it."

A very special thanks to Bobby Kirkwood and Cheryl Pitkin, who waded deep into the hours of word processing the manuscript.

Finally, last but certainly not least, my loving family, my wife Karen Mills-Alston and daughter Lindsay, who endured the frantic schedule, tolerated my absence, and labored through the transition. To my parents who have always been there, my mother Bette Cox, and my father John Alston; sister Carole, stepfather Jim Cox, Herman and Pauline Yarbrough, Lois and Beatrice Crawford. Uncle Gary Brown, you were right when you said, "Fill your cup and keep filling it, for only when it is full enough will it begin to overflow."

Thank you, and I thank God.
J.A.

A special thanks to my mother, the first author in my family, my sister, Tamra, who encouraged me to continue writing, and my niece Amy, a promising young writer, who offered me a teen's view of this work. I am grateful to my children, Carolyn and Mark Junior, and particularly, H. P., my adolescent, with whom I rebonded during the creation of this book. Finally, I would like to thank the Reverend Doctor Mark Richardson, my partner for life, who taught me that learning must always continue.

B.L.R

CONTENTS

PART II

NEW BEGINNINGS

PART III

MOVING TOWARD NEW LIVES

INTRODUCTION

I was visiting a childhood friend a while back, and we were chatting over mugs of coffee, when her 16-year-old son returned from school. Even if we had wanted to, it would have been difficult to ignore him. His sullenness pervaded the room. He's a tall, handsome young man, but as I stood to greet him, I noticed his appearance. His sneakers were unlaced, his tee shirt hung from beneath an athletic jacket, his beltless pants seemed poised to drop at a moment's notice, and his shoulder-length hair hung from beneath a cap.

Still, I was delighted to see him. His mother and I had grown up on the same block and attended neighborhood schools together. We'd kept in touch as we moved away to separate colleges, and eventually, into our respective marriages and our roles as parents. Despite the geographical distance, I'd always thought of her son as my nephew. It didn't take long to realize that Junior didn't share my feelings. Although I'd extended my hand in greeting, his fists remained tucked inside his pockets.

His mother spoke with forced cheerfulness. "No hats in the house, please. You remember Uncle John, don't you, dear?"

He grunted something that sounded like "Yeah, what's up?" and headed up the stairs munching a stack of chips.

At that point, I saw fire in my old friend's eyes, and I understood what she felt. Based upon what we'd been taught 30 years before, while growing up in our tightly knit Los Angeles neighborhood, Junior was sorely lacking in manners. No matter how much she and I may

1

have complained about the "establishment" back then, we wouldn't have considered being rude to our parents or their friends.

Before I could say a word, my friend had raced up the steps behind Junior. Although she began talking calmly, her voice soon rose to a shout, so I couldn't avoid overhearing most of what she said: "As long as you live . . . that attitude . . . want me to slap . . . ashamed of yourself. . . ." I heard every word she was saying . . . I wonder if Junior did.

I sat there listening, but not in judgement, for who could swear they'd never be in a similar situation? I couldn't resist thinking, however, that if I'd been given a crystal ball just a few hours earlier, and known what was going to happen, I could have written in advance the words she was now using to scold her son. That's how predictable and familiar her monologue seemed. In fact she and I both could have written the script together, three decades before. The words seemed lifted from pages of our shared history. For she and I, like most of our contemporaries, had heard grown-ups talk like that throughout our childhoods.

When my friend returned to the kitchen, she looked defeated. "I've given him everything," she said, and I knew she meant it. Few parents could be better intentioned than this woman and her husband. They'd sent their son to the best schools, worked hard to live in a safe, comfortable neighborhood, and had lots of family time together, including regular church attendance and long summer vacations.

She began wringing her hands while she spoke. "He's like that with teachers, too, and he never gets any chores done. I can't even get him to keep his hat off. He's rotten to the core. I don't know how he's going to survive out there. I try to explain to him that life won't be this comfortable unless he shows some motivation. But he doesn't even understand the connection between effort and reward. He just assumes that when he grows up he'll be successful. All he cares about is having fun, now."

She paused for a minute, shaking her head, then continued. "I tell you, if I had known what to expect I would never have had kids. I'd have volunteered to help other people crazy enough to have them. Every mother I know feels the same way." After a moment of silence, she looked up at me hopefully. "What do you think? You were a therapist. You travel all over the country talking to kids. Your cousin saw you talk to 1,000 teenagers, and he said when the lunch bell rang they didn't budge from their seats. How did you get through to them?"

I had a lot of answers that day, but none of them were five minute solutions. Quick fixes would have been impossible even when the world was far simpler, when we'd been raised to live, worship, and think the way our parents did, and when, despite our sixties rebellion, we'd allowed our parents' values to define our futures.

My friend looked frightened, and for good reason. Those times we lived in are gone forever. We are the parents now. Many of us are raising our children in the most comfortable of circumstances. But we cannot ignore the turbulence of the times. We must prepare our children to face a host of moral dilemmas, and not preparing them might be too costly.

The Children's Defense Fund recently published these frightening and grim statistics: Every seven seconds in America a child is arrested for a drug offense. Every eight seconds of the school day, a child drops out. Every 26 seconds, a child runs away from home. Every 67 seconds, a child gives birth. Every 30 minutes, one is arrested for drunken driving. Every 36 minutes, one is killed or injured by a gun. These are times that call for aggressive parenting, for a novel approach to getting through to our teenagers, because raising them is not a lottery game. We can't just leave their futures to chance.

I've written this book for my dear old friend, who I hope will forgive the long pause between her questions and my response; and for all the parents who've "given their kids everything," but still don't know how best to communicate with them. This is a book for parents who wonder how we can give young people what we really want them to take when they leave our homes as full grown adults: a sense of purpose in this world, honesty and strength of character, a drive to succeed and the savvy to stay on top once they get there.

Story Power conveys a new approach to communicating with teens. It is about listening to stories that they bring to us, as they attempt to thrive and survive.

Story Power is a way to understand what they are telling us and tell them what we want, so they can truly comprehend.

The core of a story well expressed can mold thinking and serve as a guide for behavior, so this communication tool I call "story power" can develop strong character, integrity, and decency in the young adults we are nurturing. Children will become older no matter what we, as parents and concerned adults, do to influence them. The influence we provide is crucial to the kind of adults they become.

And what do our teenagers want from us? Well, I was in St. Paul, Minnesota last week, and talked to a young woman—one of thousands of teenagers whom I meet each month—whose words still ring in my ears. "When you look closely," she said, "nobody really cares about us or wants to know what we have to say or even listens."

I told her, "We grown-ups must have been doing something wrong if we've given you that impression. I know adults care, that's why we keep trying to get through to you. We do want you to hear us, but we also want to listen to you."

Story power is not only a tool for understanding and responding to the way teens are experiencing their lives, it is a means of coming to terms with our own present experiences, relationships, personal dramas, and events that we have lived out. Story power is *remembering* so that, in communicating with teens, we can speak honestly, and listen with an open, discerning ear.

So, parents, teachers, it's up to us. We must try a new way of communicating with this generation of youngsters raised to expect it all. Because no matter how great our hopes for them, or how generous our contribution, they'll never hear us unless we learn to stop sounding like broken records. In turbulent times such as these, there are better ways to get their attention and teach them what we want them to know.

This book is not a panacea, nor a quick fix. It is just one additional approach to consider as we strive to build resilient, competent, good, decent human beings.

I

THE
CONVINCING
POWER OF
OUR
STORIES
AND WHY KIDS
NEED THEM

1

What We Want For Our Children

A Quiz For Adults

I've found that the only fun quizzes are the ones we can take knowing, with absolute certainty, that we will pass. So herewith, a quiz you can enjoy. Give yourself five points for each of the phrases listed below that you or your partner may have used when talking to your teenager.

Can't you do anything right?
What's wrong with you? (or) Are you crazy?
How many times do I have to tell you?
This room looks like a pigpen.
Do you want me to slap you?
Are you happy now?
Don't ask why, just do it!
Wait until you have children of your own.
Now, that was just stupid.
Aren't you ashamed of yourself? (or) You should be ashamed of yourself.
As long as you're in my house . . .
When I was your age . . .
You're old enough to know better.
I hate to say it, but I told you so.

7

You won't listen to me.
You got just what you deserve.
This is going to hurt me more than it hurts you.
This is for your own good.
I'm doing this all for you.
After all I've done for you.
Why don't you just stop lying.
This is inexcusable.
There's nothing you can say.
Who do you think you're talking to?
Sure. . . .
Because I said so, that's why.
I'm going to tell you this one more time . . .
I don't care what the other kids are doing.
What have I done to deserve this?
Where did I go wrong?
You've got to be kidding.
Read my lips.

So, you scored some points? All the adults I tested did also. One friend had used *all* of the phrases. I didn't give him a long drawn out lecture about using them, and I'm not going to scold you about them either. You probably hate being lectured to just as much as your kids do. And just like your kids, you wouldn't listen anyway.

I do suggest, however, that you photocopy this list, hang it on your refrigerator and consider it your first step to launching a new relationship with your teenager. It can be an amusing start for turning your lives around. Tell your teenager you don't want to use these phrases anymore, to remind you when you do, and to feel free to add any to the list which I might have left out.

Why Kids Don't Listen

You'll find more at the end of this chapter that I hadn't even remembered myself, but which kids say they hear at home. I've surveyed hundreds of teenagers about their parents' communication styles. I'll be sharing some of what they had to say throughout the book.

I call these phrases "parentisms"—words we use in moments of exasperation, when we simply can't think of anything else. It's important to begin with something that seems as simple as these phrases because it's essential to remove these old barriers between you and your adolescent. They are signals to our teenagers. It's as if our kids suddenly see a big puff of smoke over our heads, like the balloons drawn over comic book characters. But unlike cartoons, our balloons always contain the same messages to our kids: "You can stop listening here. This is more of the continuing series on responsibility, maturity, good hygiene, neatness, hard work . . . blah, blah, blah." No greater barrier to communicating with our teenagers exists than these parentisms. And they are often the reason young people don't listen.

Deciding What You Want

One family I read about recently sent the following announcement to friends:

Mr. & Mrs. Thomas Wilson
announce the birth of their son
Dr. Thomas Wilson III
January 5, 1991
7 lbs., 4 ozs.

I hope the future "Dr. Thomas Wilson III," will have a good laugh about it someday. But when the laughter ends, what will his parents really tell him about what they expect from him? What do you say to your child? Do you have a clear vision of what you hope he will be like?

My only problem with parents listing "success" at the top of their list of aspirations is that something quite important seems to have been left out. How about old fashioned goodness—being honest, fair, caring, trustworthy and kind—and what about helping those who are less fortunate?

Take a look at the world around us. Look at our greatest colleges and universities, where administrators are forced to deal with the issues of cheating and date rape. Look at Wall Street, where the "best and brightest" were dragged before television cameras and courts of law to face charges for financial irregularities. The list is endless but the point remains the same. We must present our children with a clear message about what we expect of them and instill in them a sense of how they can make a difference.

Your teenager's future is determined by parental input and events that, sometimes, are completely out of your control. Unless you have clear and definable dreams for your adolescent, you are like an unconditioned, unprepared athlete on a playing field. There are lots of big guys from the other team, racing at you, determined to knock you down, causing you to fail as a parent. That's how powerful outside influences can be.

Let's indulge in dreams for a minute. Right now, take time to decide, specifically, what you want for your child. Formulate it in your mind. What is she like years from now? How is she contributing her talents to this world? Now try to picture your teenager becoming that adult. If you can't imagine it, draw a picture or simply sketch a box on a piece of paper, and fill in those goals. (If you still can't imagine any of this don't give up. Before this book is over, you'll feel differently.)

With dreams, you've got something to aim for. Plant them in your mind, hang them over your bed, your desk, wherever necessary, to remind yourself that, in future dealings, what you say and do regarding your teenager will make a difference in whether or not he understands and believes that he can grow into a caring and strong adult who can change the future for many others. With that vision in mind, let's move on. There are unlimited prospects ahead.

What Teens Say:
Parents Say The Darndest Things

NOTE TO PARENTS: At the end of chapters 1 through 8, you will find feedback I've collected from 469 teenagers from around the country, ages 14 through 19. Each new sentence represents a different voice. You may want to read these pages to develop a feel for what other teenagers and their parents are doing and saying. You may then find that your youngster enjoys reading these sections and discussing the feelings, ideas, and events that are expressed.

- "I suppose if someone jumped off a bridge you would too."
- "As long as you live under my roof . . ."
- "Are you addicted to that phone, or something?"
- "Do you think I'm made out of money?"
- "You're not going to wear that, are you?"
- "You're wasting my time."
- "I'm disappointed in you."
- "Shut up!"
- "How could you do something so stupid!"
- "It doesn't matter what you think."
- "I thought you were smarter than that."
- "I never did that when I was a kid."
- "You must do what I say, you don't have a choice."
- "I didn't raise you that way."
- "I wish you'd been a boy."
- "I hate you."
- "You don't know what you're talking about."
- "Now that was just stupid."
- "You're going to make me do something drastic."
- "We do everything for you."
- "You think you know it all, don't you?"
- "Just who do you think you are?"
- "I can't trust you with anything."
- "Cut the crap."
- "We never had it as easy as you."
- "If you don't act like an adult how do you expect to be treated like one?"
- "There will be no discussion. Do as I say!"

- "I've said it before and I'll say it again."
- "How come it's only an A minus?"
- "Because you're a girl."
- "I would never have said that to my mother."
- "Act your age."
- "You'll always be my little baby, no matter how old you get."
- "I'm the parent, you're the child, that's why."
- "Don't make me say this again."
- "Do whatever you want—why did you bother to ask?"
- "Is that the best you can do?"
- "You've let me down."
- "Life is tough."
- "Shape up!"
- "So and so has never done that."
- "You're always doing something wrong."
- "I'm only looking out for your best interests."
- "Don't roll your eyes at me."
- "I thought I could trust you."
- "You are a failure."
- "I'm ashamed of you."
- "You're just like your father."
- "You're so irresponsible."
- "I don't want to hear one more word from you."
- "I don't care what other parents let their kids do."
- "Stop lying!"
- "I don't want anything to do with you anymore."
- "This is my house."
- "You're lazy."
- "You're worthless."
- "Just who do you think you are?"
- "Don't talk back to me, young lady."
- "You have it too easy."
- "You have a bad attitude."
- "All you think about is yourself."
- "You don't appreciate anything we do."
- "Don't tell me how to be a mother."
- "You're only a kid."
- "If you don't like the way things are going, leave!"
- "You don't have to listen to me, but '. . . '"
- "I brought you into this world and I can take you out."
- "Why can't you be more like your sister?"

- "You'd better be careful because I'm watching your every move."
- "Don't talk (when I'm yelling at you)."
- "You'll look back on this and see I'm right."
- "I'm the man in this house."
- "You're jinxed."
- "You'll be sorry."
- "Grow up!"
- "Then go live with your father."
- "One day you'll thank me for this."
- "You'll never be able to do that."
- "What's wrong, don't you want to learn?"
- "Do you want to be stupid the rest of your life?"

These comments are often troublesome to a teenager. Although the person saying them may have good intentions, they can be interpreted in a variety of ways. Generally, however, they seem to be designed to do one or all of the following:

Motivate the teenager to change for the better;

Express our anger or frustration;

Get the teenager to recognize and respect authority.

When I am asked the question, "What do I want for our children?" my answer is always the same. More than anything else, I want them to venture forth on the path to decency. I want them to grow into adults who care about others; adults who want to be honest and fair; adults who despise cruelty, suffering and who choose to give to everyone what they want the most . . . respect and kind regard. We need adult models who relate to teens in a way that they will listen. And we need better stories in which they can believe, stories that move them to do the right thing, to be a better person and treat others the way we all want to be treated—with respect and dignity.

Let's look at 2 more effective ways of communicating.

2

The Power of a Story and How To Use It

When I first heard of Pat and Lisa Stringer, I must say I was pretty dismayed by their behavior. But as I've come to know the family, I have begun to feel that this is an important story to share with you. It seems particularly apropos in light of the fact that the teenagers I've talked to rated sex as first on their list of subjects they can't discuss with their parents. This story is enough to jolt any parent into reconsidering how to communicate with a teenager. It begins with a shock, but ends with a measure of hope for us all.

A Shocking Incident
And a New Beginning

Once a month for the last few years, Pat Stringer, who lives with her family on one of the Florida Keys, has hosted sorority luncheons in her flower-filled atrium. Stringer was recently smack in the middle of one of these affairs when she was interrupted by her 16-year-old daughter, Lisa. To Pat, it was obvious from the look on the blonde cheerleader's face that she had something important to say. But rather than weave her way between the two card tables and speak in a whisper, Lisa stood in the doorway and bellowed across the room: "Mom, where did you put the condoms?"

Pat told me later, "It was like a bad joke. I wanted to clear the room and slap her. I was humiliated. It's not as if my sorority sisters

15

don't understand that teenagers act irrationally, sometimes, but this was like a deliberate attempt to hurt me. I kept wondering, why? What had I done to deserve this kind of treatment? My friends had always said we were more like sisters than mother and daughter."

Two weeks before, Pat felt she had put what she considered their "already solid relationship" on a new and more mature footing. She had discovered Lisa's panties in the den, wedged between some couch cushions. Stringer panicked, realizing that only the night before, she'd left Lisa and her boyfriend in the same spot, where they'd been watching TV.

"Then I stopped and thought it through," Stringer said. "I felt I had to choose between trying to prevent my daughter from having a sexual relationship, which probably would have been impossible, or accepting the inevitable and encouraging her to protect herself."

Pat talked it over with her husband, then decided to buy a box of condoms for Lisa. She told her that while she wasn't condoning teenage sex, at least she hoped her daughter would protect herself from the possibilities of disease and pregnancy. Lisa had thanked her. "It was a difficult moment for me, but I felt so close to her," Stringer continued. "I wish my mother and I could have talked on this level. And I was proud of myself, of my calmness rather than hysteria, because my insides were rioting. It couldn't have been very different from the way mothers feel when they send their children off to war. But as far as I was concerned, it was a conversation that might have saved her life."

Lisa had chirped a polite thank you and was off, supposedly for a shopping trip.

"That was it," Stringer said. "I didn't bring it up again, but boy, was I furious! I didn't mention it because I didn't know what to say. I realized she was testing me. And I especially didn't want my original message obscured. I don't like the idea of Lisa having sex with this kid. For goodness sake, she's just a kid herself. But I can't control every minute of her life anymore than any parent could. We could have gotten caught up in accusations and explanations and also we could have lost sight of the fact that I don't want my daughter to get pregnant or to die from AIDS."

Try for a moment to imagine yourself in Stringer's shoes. Your kid has just pulled an emotional quick switch and you're furious. Granted, this is an unusual situation, but a parent being embarrassed by a teenager is not. How would you have handled Lisa's outburst? Would you have:

a) Desperately attempted to convince your guests they'd misunderstood, by saying to Lisa, "You know Mr. and Mrs. Conder are on vacation."
b) Refused to play along and dumped your luncheon plate over her head.
c) Said, while smiling through clenched teeth, "Do you really think this is the time or place to discuss a subject like that?"
d) Risen from your seat and said firmly, "Go to your room right now, young lady! We'll talk when my guests are gone. (Once she has crept away you might try humming theme music from the movie, "Rocky.")
e) Excused yourself, asked Lisa to follow you to another room where you would have given her a good smack across the face, and/or told her off. ("How dare you act that way! After all I've done for you.")
f) Done exactly as Pat did, who on that sunny afternoon found herself humiliated in the middle of the atrium, her sorority sisters in stunned silence. Her first thought was to try to save face, she later said. She did, temporarily at least, by calmly responding to her daughter's inquiry, "Don't you remember, dear, they're in your bathroom cabinet, where we left them."

Let's face it, these options are severely limited. Most are downright ridiculous and none address the real problem. Even Pat admitted that her tactic left her seething. That meant two people were furious, Lisa and her mother. I think it's pretty obvious Lisa was angry about something. She'd stood boldly in the doorway and embarrassed her mother, in front of friends. And what did Pat do? She responded with a smile. What were her choices? If she had lashed out at Lisa, it wouldn't have been effective. Either way, they would have avoided talking about what was really happening.

A New Way of Communicating

I'd like to suggest a simple alternative, one that addresses Pat's feelings in a gentle but forceful manner, and at the same time offers the opportunity for the two to really talk. This alternative, my method for communicating with teenagers, has already been mastered by many parents whom I've met in workshops, that I've conducted around the country for the past decade. Using Pat and Lisa as models, I'll present the six steps you'll need to know, then I'll give you a detailed explanation.

1. Take the child aside for a conversation, even if only for a few minutes.
2. Use the three Cs—Concentrate, Catch reckless words before they come out, and get yourself under Control.
3. Seize control of the moment by setting the tone.
4. Set up a time to talk about what has happened.
5. Before the appointment, spend time thinking about an incident in your life that you can share with your child to get the conversation on the right footing.
6. Share your story with your child.
7. Don't expect sudden change. Allow your message to sink in.

   Using the Stringers to illustrate:

1. Excuse yourself from the room. Pat could have told her guests she had to speak to her daughter privately. Changing location often gives you time to calm down, just a bit, and think. It can also remove you from the inquiring eyes of your audience. When "outsiders" are in the vicinity, parents tend to dispense discipline to please the crowd, rather than in the child's best interests.
2. Force yourself, for the first few minutes, to keep quiet, even if this means counting to yourself. Reining in your anger is not easy. But you have probably also learned that reckless words cannot be taken back. As someone once said, you can't unpop popcorn. Once angry words begin flying, they can lead you where you don't want to go.

       En route to the new location, remind yourself of the goals you have in mind for your child. This is another calming-down routine. Pat has told me that she hopes Lisa will turn out to be a "caring, loving adult." Whatever you're hoping for, try to keep that picture fixed in your mind. It can be especially helpful before you speak.
3. When you are finally face-to-face, seize the moment by setting the tone. Begin with something neutral and to the point: for example, "We need to talk." A statement like this works because it does not address your rage. Save that for later, when you're able to exert more self-control. Remember, the greatest difference between adults and teenagers is that we're supposed to be the mature ones. That means our actions are not always ruled by our emotions.
4. Take out a calendar or date book. Set up a specific time, preferably only a few hours from then (even less is better), to discuss what has

happened. Don't allow yourself to be pulled into a shouting match. If your teenager is whining or yelling something to the effect of, "What's wrong? What'd I do? Why won't you tell me?" remain firm. Repeat again that you want to talk, and agree on a time.

If you have any reason to believe that she might skip the appointment, set up consequences. Say something to the effect of, "This is important. I have to insist that if you cannot make the appointment at the time we've agreed upon, you must do without telephone calls, television, dates, or distractions of any kind, until we've agreed on a new time and you follow through on it."

Even if you don't have a roomful of people waiting for you, or if no pressing engagement looms, this tactic gives you time to think about what you're going to say. Making an appointment also sends a powerful but unspoken message to your teenager. It says: "I am treating you in a respectful manner, which is the same way I would like to be treated. Also, your actions were inappropriate and must be dealt with." And most importantly, you're saying that your feelings count.

Consider the beauty of it. You're able to say all this without being pulled into an emotional mud fight.

5. Before the appointment, devote a few minutes to recalling an experience that will frame a suitable story to tell your child.

Calling on Her Own Story

No "Hansel and Gretel" or "Cinderella" here. These are stories that you may never have realized were there, right in your head. They are so powerful, so necessary, that you'll wonder how you ever planned to raise a teenager without using them.

Let me give you an illustration. I asked Pat to try and recall some incident that had occurred in her own life that might help Lisa. Her immediate response was typical. She said, "I can't imagine a thing I could tell her from my own experience. I would never have done that to my mother." Of course you wouldn't have, I told her. So what's new about that? That, I advised her, would not have been a good start to this conversation with Lisa. Pat laughed, realizing she'd just repeated one of her favorite parentisms.

I tried backing up a bit and urged Pat to trust me because I was not only certain she could do this, but I knew her relationship with Lisa depended on her mastery of story power. I tried to help Pat recall an event in her life which, at the time, might have seemed minor. As she continued resisting, I paraphrased a quote by the writer Flannery O'Connor that anyone who has ever survived childhood has enough stories to last for a lifetime.

I told her that O'Connor, when asked about some of the exaggerated images in her short stories, said something else we'd do well to remember: "To the hard of hearing you shout," she said, "and for the almost-blind you draw large and startling figures." We might well add, "and for teenagers numbed by lectures and sermons, parents must create stories so vital, their kids can see and feel what they're saying.

Like many parents trying this method for the first time, Pat seemed stuck. I suggested another tactic. "Let's go back to that day at the luncheon," I said. "Lisa's in the doorway shouting across the room. Tell me, how did you feel?"

"Humiliated!" Pat yelled.

"Well then, give it some thought," I said. "Those stories are there in your mind, listed under your humiliation file. Start turning through the old manila folders . . . quickly . . . faster. Toss some ideas out and let me hear them. The memories are waiting for you. How about when you were young, say in your young teens or pre-teens. At that age you're almost embarrassed to be alive. Even eating in front of someone of the opposite sex can be miserable. You might have a piece of sauerkraut hanging from your teeth or bread pudding on your lip. Did you fall walking down an aisle at church, or maybe slip on graduation day? What was it?"

Pat began giggling. "I just thought of something," she said, and she blushed, pausing.

I waited, wanting to pull the story out of her. "What was it?"

"It was nothing," she said.

"Go ahead, tell me," I said, "you're still embarrassed about it."

"It's just that it was so silly."

In the end, I had to almost drag it out of her, but as she told me of the incident, I saw a flicker of understanding in her eyes. In fact, I was so certain she had chosen the perfect story, I suggested she offer it to Lisa, although the "condoms" incident was weeks old.

She did, and because I want to give you a clear picture of what occurred when she spoke with Lisa, I have tried to give a full account, according to Pat, of their conversation. This occurred at Pat and Lisa's appointment.

PAT: There's something I wanted to tell you, something that hap-
       pened in my life which I'd almost forgotten. I started thinking
       about it after my sorority luncheon.

LISA: This isn't about something that I did wrong, is it?

PAT: May I share this with you?

LISA: (Bending her head, sighing with resignation) I guess.

PAT: It happened when I was thirteen.

LISA: What?

PAT: Maybe someone gave it to me, I don't know.

LISA: Gave you what?

PAT: It was a two-piece bathing suit.

LISA: (Laughing, a bit maliciously) You?

PAT: Yup, as chubby as I was, I wore it. I don't know where my
       parents were, maybe it was during the summer. They weren't
       around.

LISA: Maybe you were cutting school.

PAT: (She shrugs) I do remember the beach though. It was Riis in
       Brooklyn.

LISA: Yuck! That place you showed me that time.

PAT: Um hm. I was interested in boys and there were lots of them out
       that day. I went in the water . . .

LISA: You can't swim.

PAT: (Laughing) You think I don't remember that? Well, I must have
       been frolicking, as we called it in those days. Somehow I got in
       pretty deep and I remember the water being up to my neck. A
       big wave must have come along because I went under. I wasn't
       worried about drowning or anything, maybe the person I was
       with helped me regain my footing. Isn't it strange? I have no
       idea who might have been there. Anyway, my point is that by
       the time I was standing again, I'd lost my bathing suit top.

LISA: (Gasping with her hand over brace-filled mouth) Stop!

PAT: And at some point I had to get out of the water. You'd think the
       person I was with would have just gone and found something
       for me to put on. I don't know. So, I got out of the water, with
       my hands over my breasts. They were never really that
       big . . .

LISA: Oh my G . . .

PAT: (Shaking her head knowingly) The fact that they were so small
       was probably part of my embarrassment. I mean if you're going
       to come out of the water bare breasted, when you're 13, you
       want to look like . . .

LISA: Madonna?

PAT: Yeah. But at least not like a chubby Pee Wee Herman.

LISA: So what happened?

PAT: Nothing anyone on that beach probably remembers. A few boys might have tittered. One of them might have even walked over and pointed while he was laughing. But as I'm telling you this story it seems to me, now, that everyone on Pier Five was laughing. I've blocked out a lot of the details, or maybe it's just that it was so long ago, but the embarrassment remains.

LISA: Oh, I would have died.

PAT: I wanted to . . . But I told you that story for a reason. When I was remembering it the other day, I was able to look at it through my adult eyes. It's not surprising I was embarrassed. Anyone would have been, regardless of age. But because I was 13 and overweight and unsure of myself . . . and then it was that time, too. You didn't see women with almost no clothes on television or in magazines. Forget showing models in bras and Brigitte Bardot was a scandal . . .

LISA: Who's . . .

PAT: My point is that we were taught to think of our bodies as something you kept covered until that one special man came along. Your body was something sacred.

LISA: I get it. You've changed your mind about this sex thing.

PAT: I wish I were better at this. But I'd like you to hear me out. Well, the other day, at the luncheon when you walked in and mentioned, in front of everyone, about the condoms, I felt the same way I did on that beach that day. I wondered why, and so I had to think about it . . . Then I understood. Our conversation about you having sex with Phillip, and the act of sex itself, is something sacred to me.

LISA: Oh, Mom.

PAT: And I felt you were exposing it to everyone in that room.

LISA: Oh . . . (long pause) I'm sorry.

PAT: Thank you for the apology. I'm going to take a moment and really feel it. (She's quiet for a few seconds, then reaches over and holds Lisa's hand. She begins shaking her head in affirmation.) That feels good. But what I want most from you is some understanding about why you were so angry with me. You must have thought I'd yell back at you, the way I did in front of your school that time.

LISA: I wasn't really . . .

PAT: Maybe if we talk about how you felt, I can understand.

I must momentarily interrupt Pat and Lisa. Often, conversations like these simply end, without resolution. In that case, the next step can be all the more important.

Accept that the telling of your personal narrative won't necessarily bring about an instant solution, or even a sense of peace. Change or resolution can require days, weeks, months. That does not diminish the deep level of rapport that has been established. If this is to be the end of the conversation for a while, acknowledge it, and thank your teenager for participating. You can feel assured that you've given her something to really think about.

Pat and Lisa made an important connection there. Pat communicated her sense of humiliation. She helped Lisa to understand that she has feelings worthy of respect. Lisa's acknowledgment indicates a level of understanding.

Why Narratives Are Important

Whether it's the first, second, or however many times you've shared a personal narrative with your teenager, be prepared for her to start opening up to you in a new way. Often, what you hear may startle you, as was the case with Pat, which brings us to that very unexpected conclusion I talked about. It turned out that Lisa had been holding back some vital information.

LISA: You're right. I was angry that day, with everybody. I was going to meet Phillip and I knew what would happen. He'd been pushing me to go all the . . . (long pause, with her head hung)
PAT: I don't understand.
LISA: Well, I haven't, um done anything. He wants me to, but . . .
PAT: You mean, no intercourse?
LISA: Right. When you saw the panties you thought I had. At first I was glad when you said it was okay.
PAT: I didn't say that.
LISA: You bought me the condoms. I thought it didn't matter to you whether I did or not and since he really wanted to . . .
PAT: Do you want to?
LISA: (Long pause) Not really.

PAT: Oh, honey, I'm so sorry. I just assumed. And you thought . . .

LISA: No, you thought, Mom.

PAT: (Embracing her.) I did. I jumped the gun, so why don't I just shut up now and let you finish.

LISA: I guess I just wanted you to say 'no,' that you'd kill me or something and then I coulda just told him no. But . . . (she begins crying)

PAT: You really thought I didn't care?

LISA: Yes.

PAT: About?

LISA: Me.

PAT: I am sorry. I care very much. I'm relieved that you haven't. I'm glad. You're such a strong girl. But that's what you are, you're still a girl, and we've all been forcing you to be something else. It must have been so difficult so say no, but I'm so proud that you had the strength to do what is right—even though I let you down.

LISA: I love you Mom.

PAT: I know. I love you. I'm glad we talked.

I'd like to take the time to thank Pat and Lisa, as well as all the families you will meet, for their openness. I'll reflect on what occurred in this final installment of their conversation, as well as that essential piece of information that emerged. I'll also offer some ideas about why Lisa might not have told Pat about the pressure she was getting from her boyfriend. And about Pat, I'll discuss why she so hastily supplied her daughter with condoms. It's important to note that Pat was sending a confusing message. She may have believed she was telling Lisa not to have sex, and obviously had instilled in her a firm resolve against it. But by supplying her with condoms, she contradicted her own message. No matter what we tell our kids, there's a chance they will have sex before marriage anyway. One million teenage pregnancies—30 percent of all pregnancies in this country—each year prove that. Despite this, you can tell your child, in a clear and noncontradictory fashion, why you're personally opposed to teenage sex by giving the facts about the health and pregnancy risks and explaining that sexual intercourse has far reaching psychological and moral consequences, which most teenagers are not equipped to handle. Let your child know, early on, that you're open to discussing the subject but, if you've gotten off to a bad start, don't despair. More important than anything else, make your values and sentiments known to your child as early as his maturity and immediate environment allow.

The fact that Lisa was not sexually active and needed reinforcement in her resolve not to become so, might never have been disclosed, if the crisis had not prompted Pat to bring the conversation to a new level.

I've been assured by many of the adults I've worked with that the more it's practiced, the easier telling your personal narratives becomes. It's not unusual for me to talk to teenagers, with whom I've shared my stories, and have one say or write to me, "You saved my life with your stories. I was going to kill myself." These personal narratives work because they are life affirming.

Here are some tips on how to select and shape your own narratives:

1. Don't begin with the phrase, "When I was your age." It's a turn-off. If you can't think of an opening, use the words, "You know what I've been thinking about . . ."
2. Try to "match feelings," with a particular incident, as I encouraged Pat to do. She was humiliated at that luncheon, and she searched her mental file for a relevant memory.
3. Begin keeping a "memory notebook," in which you can compile any memories—good, bad, even those you may even feel indifferent about at the moment. Try working chronologically. Don't just write vague references to them, though. Try to recall details. How old were you? How did you feel? Who else was there? What might you have been wearing? What was the season; approximate time of day or night? Try to recreate dialogue. Also include memories of holidays, celebrations, vacations, rites of passage, favorite and worst gifts, siblings, childhood homes, house hunting when you married, when you were single.

   You won't necessarily be sharing all of these stories, but you'll find that once you begin recreating events, you'll begin remembering more.
4. Examples of stories or themes you can share with your child include:
   • Your heroes
   • Mentors
   • Relatives
   • Model citizens

- Teachers
- Events that changed your thinking.
- Clergy
- Fairness
- Decency
- Compassion
- Humility
- Responsibility
- The desire to learn
- Feeling lost
- Acts of cruelty, generosity or love
- The struggle to find the right solution
- Memorable fiction or nonfiction
- First traffic ticket
- Passing or failing a driving test
- Your first pet
- Favorite toy
- Best friends
- News items
- Why you decided to change something about yourself
- The worst trouble you've been in
- The worst tongue lashing from your parents
- The neighborhood bully
- Favorite television programs, movies, or plays
- How you conquered fears
- Your first kiss
- Your first crush
- A favorite music group when you were a teenager
- Where you were when Kennedy was shot, when Martin Luther King, Jr. was assassinated
- Your first heartbreak
- A religious experience
- A first day at school
- Conquering your worst habit
- Your most frightening experience
- Early memories of marriage, life with your spouse
- The death of a loved one
- A time when you said something that embarrassed or hurt someone else.

5. Remember that stories can have many purposes. For example, they can:
   - Introduce an idea
   - Convey a point of view
   - Reveal or tap into feelings
   - Instruct
   - Convey opinions, beliefs, and facts
   - Offer reasoned arguments
   - Share virtues
   - Explain positions, feelings.
6. Once you decide on a story, keep its purpose in mind. Envision yourself moving toward a finish line and make the story travel in that direction so you don't go off on a tangent. You'll be able to learn, as other parents in this book shape their stories.
7. Try to include colorful details.
8. Don't drag your story out. It should last anywhere from two to ten minutes. Pause occasionally to let your youngster ask a question or respond to a point you've made.
9. Don't strive for a big ending. Leave that to filmmakers. Try to wind up by saying something such as, "What happened here made me think about. . . ."or, "I guess it reminded me that. . . ."

As you continue to read this book, you'll discover that the stories of our lives have recurring themes, and you'll discover more and more reasons to employ them. The dramas we live through provide legacies for our children. A good story establishes a bond between the teller and listener. It bridges realities and brings people with opposing views closer together.

In the next chapter I will share more personal narratives, as well as some of my own experiences and how I learned the power of a story.

What Teens Say:
Parental Bottom Lines

"The one thing our parents absolutely , no questions asked, expect of us is . . .

(Once again, each new sentence or phrase represents a new voice.)

- "That I overachieve."
- "That I prepare for my future."
- "To shut the door of the dog pen after I clean it."
- "That the house will be clean."
- "Reasonable grades, no Cs or under."
- "I not hide my problems from them, no matter how terrible."
- "Grades no lower than 3.6"
- "That I not drink and drive."
- "Do my homework."
- "Be perfect (it seems)."
- "All As and Bs—at least a 3.8"
- "That I believe in myself."
- "That I reach all my goals."
- "Be a good example for my younger sister."
- "To take out the garbage."
- "I must mow the lawn."
- "They expect honesty and a 4 point average."
- "That I follow through on commitments."
- "That I not lie."
- "I'm not sure there is anything."
- "Participate in church activities and go to church EVERY week."
- "To do my best and do it with pride."
- "To not kill anyone."
- "Enjoy life."
- "Be respectful."
- "Go to college."
- "To be happy (no kidding)."
- "Live up to my potential."
- "That I am a good person."
- "No driving tickets."

- "Succeed in life."
- "I make the honor roll."
- "To do the impossible."
- "That I use my talents."
- "To be polite to adults."
- "That I get into UCLA or better."
- "No drugs or alcohol."
- "That I am considerate to others."
- "Good manners."
- "Go to college in Texas."
- "That I tell the truth."
- "That I get straight As."
- "That I be like my sister."
- "A clean mouth (no cursing)."
- "That I get a part-time job."
- "Act like a young lady, most of the time."
- "Be kind to others."
- "I spend one day out of the weekend with them."
- "I remain a Christian."
- "To abstain from alcohol, drugs, sex."
- "To be true to myself."
- "That I have a positive outlook."
- "That I graduate from high school."
- "My dad wants me to stay a virgin until I get married (my mother knows better than my dad)."

3

Personal
Narratives
and
Why They Work

I'm certainly not the first person to discover that personal stories have impact. Some of the best orators, including Winston Churchill, Norman Vincent Peale, Dr. Martin Luther King, Jr. and President John F. Kennedy told stories of their visions so effectively, they brought about sweeping changes in America.

As good as they were, the best speech I've ever heard didn't take place on an inaugural platform or even the pulpit of a famous church. Instead, it was delivered in a shabby tent in Los Angeles, during a revival meeting that a college buddy convinced me to attend. This preacher, whose name I cannot even recall now, was enjoying great success. Each night, several thousand people came to hear him, and when he finished speaking, at least a hundred people stood and testified each night that they'd been born again.

It was 1979, a time when polls indicated that Americans were turning away from established religions. I was curious about why this man was so successful when so many others in his field were not. I'm glad I went. But I never heard this man preach. He shared his stories, leading us along the spiritual path he'd followed. I can still hear his voice, deep and timorous, when he said, ". . . and when my foot touched that first step, I was no longer afraid to look around. I knew then and there, I could never turn back." This man knew what others had learned before him. Nothing grabs people like a genuine story.

He also helped me to recognize that there is a particular advantage to the narrative approach. He told his story effectively because only he

31

had lived it. He was not a sophisticated man. In fact, it was his very lack of polish that made his message compelling. He offered us something novel—himself, raw, and blemished.

That's what we do when we share our personal narratives with our youngsters. We offer no less than ourselves. The fact that the method works shouldn't be surprising. It has been tested by time. In centuries past, when living was less complex, more people understood the necessity of passing on narrative legacies. Though the work was often brutal—fathers toiling with sons, daughters laboring alongside their mothers—there was more time for sharing stories of failures, success, and personal codes of morality.

Of course, today's teenagers, thanks in part to child labor laws, lead vastly different lives. Their education is compulsory and they live longer, marry later, and are expected to spend time pondering life. More significantly, however, they spend precious hours staring into the great silencer—television. All these centuries later, they are still listening, but now they hear strangers' stories.

A Modern Twist

As today's parents, we can revive this story tradition, but with an updated and modern twist. Thanks to a slew of research, popular books, and television programs, many of us have come to appreciate the importance of emotional honesty. Just for the record, emotional honesty is the glue of a healthy relationship, be it familial, platonic, or romantic.

Without this sort of candor, there can be no real intimacy. Knowing this, we are encouraged not only to share the details of our stories, with our youngsters, but to set an example for them on how to express their feelings. As we weave our tales, we will not be saying, "Here's what happened to me," but, even more importantly, "and this is how I felt when it did." Nothing else will bond us with our teenagers more surely than this. Story power is the great connector.

Ironically, one of the reasons this method is so effective with today's teenagers is that we've raised them in a world that bombards them with other people's stories, from televisions shows to fan magazines. Over the years, they've learned to receive important information, in school, and in most aspects of their lives, through story-telling. The problem is that they usually know more about their favorite MTV stars or soap opera characters than they do about their parent's goals and hopes and values.

An Opportunity To Tilt the Scales

When we share our stories, we can use them to teach our values, and to develop honesty, responsibility, and strong, positive characters in our children. We are also teaching our children how to communicate with us, and with those around them. As you begin talking to your child on this new and deeper level, she will begin to feel that she truly knows you. She will understand that her experiences, dilemmas, and feelings aren't very different from yours. With that, a mutual respect will develop.

What's more, the process is self-enhancing. Anyone who has ever participated in a support group or attended a "recovery" meeting will understand this. For as we tell our stories, probing our past for the bits and pieces of our deepest emotions, we not only relive them, as people in group meetings often do, but we move one step beyond the telling. As we present them in story form we give them emotional closure.

Eunice Waters from Cleveland, who said she was always scolding her kids about wasting food, decided to share a personal narrative with them. It seems that when she was growing up, her mother had literally locked food away to keep it out of the hands of any of their paid boarders who were home during the day. It was a memory that Eunice for a long time had been unwilling to examine. She knew her mother had made many sacrifices to support her, including leaving early in the morning for an office job that lasted until late in the evening.

Eunice had grown so weary of nagging her kids about the same subject ("Clean your plate. Stop wasting food"), that she was willing to discuss her past with her teenage sons.

"When I was a kid and came home from school," she told them, "I was hungry and there were often strangers in the house, and there was nothing to eat. Everything was locked up, even the refrigerator."

Her 15-year-old son wasn't impressed. "Oh, come on, Mom. Do we have to listen to another 'when I was your age' story?" She realized that if she ever hoped to get her message across, she'd have to stop sounding trite and really reconstruct how she had felt. Then she brought the subject up again, but on a deeper level.

"I began to associate the lack of food with discomfort, with being cold and lonely, and with feeling unloved," she told them. And this time, the boys seemed to hear her and tried to change. But her own story had an impact on her, too. She started taking a closer look at her food purchases.

"There was enough extra food to last us through six months of disasters. I'd really gone overboard," she said. "Food had been my way of showing my boys that I love them. But it backfired on me. There was so much, they couldn't appreciate it. I had offered love in cookie jars and English muffins and bags of chips. When they only nibbled at it or left it out to grow stale, or for the dog to get, I was hurt."

She came to an important conclusion. "I realized that splurging on groceries would not change my past. It couldn't transport me back to a house where I would find my mother home and waiting for me. It couldn't unlock the cabinets, and it sure couldn't make me feel my mother had loved me."

"I told my kids," she continued, "that I didn't want them to judge my love according to whether or not I gave them good snacks. We laughed about it but they knew I was serious, and I began to cut back on the grocery shopping to just what I knew we would eat."

I'm glad they were able to laugh together. There's certainly no rule dictating that a narrative has to leave you feeling sad, or for that matter, has to be built around unpleasant memories. They might well be humorous, exhilarating, even mysterious.

One Father's History Lesson

One father, Alex Jacobs, whom I'd worked with, took one story and worked magic with it. He'd decided that he was going to stop fighting with his 14-year-old son, Cliff, about homework. So one evening, when the boy was complaining about an essay he had to write on Dr. King's experiences, this father reached into his memory bank and spun a story.

He said that when he was 14, his dream was to march beside Dr. King on one of his freedom marches. In fact, he said, he'd even saved his allowance and bought a ticket for a bus trip that his youth group was taking to Dr. King's church. But at the last minute, Alex said, "Mama refused to let me attend. She was afraid I'd get hurt. I'd have given anything to go."

"By the time I was old enough to go without Mama's permission," this father concluded, "Dr. King was dead. I think about that every time I see one of those old filmstrips of his 'I Have a Dream' speech." Alex had woven the nation's history into his own, and made it real for Cliff. And it worked. The boy began writing with a new found burst of energy. I'm sure you'll agree, as his teachers did, that his approach to the subject was unique.

Perhaps you've heard of Dr. King's *Letters From a Birmingham Jail*, which became the bible of the Civil Rights Movement. Well, this young man pretended that he had an opportunity to march with Dr. King and was jailed along with him. As his assignment, he wrote his own letter from the Birmingham jailhouse. Let me share just a few lines with you, from this remarkable and imaginary account:

". . . The police chief, Bull Connor, told us to stop, but Dr. King told us to keep marching, not to fight back, and to keep singing. We sang "Swing Low Sweet Chariot," and all of a sudden there was a scramble and I got pushed back by the water from the hoses and a policeman hit me with a stick. I got a big bruise on my chest and a cut on my head. I was thrown into a bus with about 100 other kids. Next thing I know, I was here.

"I'm in the cell right upstairs from Dr. King, and last night I heard him praying. He said, 'God, I thank you for these children. They give me the strength I need to break down the walls of prejudice.' When I heard him, I felt happy because I knew he was talking about us kids.

"In a way, I'm glad I came. Already we can see changes between whites and blacks. We can eat in the same restaurants and go to the same bathrooms now. I know more things will change eventually. Your loving son."

Could Alex ever have predicted the outcome of his story? I'm sure he could not have, especially because this young man's letter took on a life of its own. Let me tell you how.

The boy's letter was so well-received by his teachers, that it was nominated for an area-wide oratorical contest. He was asked to recite his letter aloud, through two preliminary rounds, and if he survived that, he would qualify for the finals.

But like most youngsters, Cliff wasn't eager to stand in front of an audience and speak. He didn't mention anything about the competition to his parents until late one night. He told his dad he didn't want to participate, but that his teacher told him he had to.

Alex wanted the boy to at least try, but he knew insisting that he do so wouldn't work. He promised his son that the next morning, before he went to work, he'd stop at the school and tell the teacher it was unfair to be forced to participate. Or, he said, if Cliff decided he wanted to do it, he would help the boy memorize it and practice it aloud. "I'm too nervous," his son argued.

"Of course you are," the father said. "The first time I made a speech I thought I was going to throw up."

The boy looked up hopefully. "Did you feel better afterwards?"

"No," his father said, "not for a long time. I really made a fool out of myself."

The boy shook his head. "Yeah, I can just see the kids at my school when I'm reading. They'll be laughing and making faces. I'm not going to do it."

The decision made, Alex was about to give up, but by now he truly believed a story might make the difference. Let me share their conversation with you.

ALEX: Let's just say that when you grow up you become . . . what would you like to be?

CLIFF: I don't know.

ALEX: If you could be anything.

CLIFF: A linebacker for the Giants.

ALEX: Okay, the Giants have just won the Superbowl. You're back in town for the ticker tape parade. Just before you leave to join your team, you get a phone call. It's from your best friend, Sam. You haven't seen him in years.

CLIFF: And?

ALEX: He's crying, tells you his son is sick, needs open heart surgery but that the doctors won't operate on the boy until he raises more money. He knows you're busy, you've got the parade and all. But he's wondering if, when the news people interview you live, that afternoon, you'd make an appeal, tell the world about his son. Would you do it for him?

CLIFF: No. I'd tell him I don't like talking in public but that I'd give him all the money I had. I'd be rich.

ALEX: But your money is tied up in investments and by the time you get your hands on it, it might be too late.

CLIFF: I don't know what I'd do.

ALEX: I don't know, either. Because, you see, it might depend on whether or not you had practiced talking in front of lots of people before, like you could do tomorrow. You'd know that even if your teammates laughed at you, it wouldn't kill you.

Cliff walked out of the room, his shoulders slumped, and Alex accepted that he had failed but was glad he had tried a story anyway.

But a few minutes later there was a knock on his bedroom door. Cliff wanted to practice. He'd decided to enter the competition, after all. And, he eventually made it to the finals. Competing against kids who loved public speaking, who'd memorized simple poems and quotes, he delivered aloud his two-page letter. He wasn't the best there. He was nervous, shaking, and forgot a lot of the lines. But the judges, admiring his chutzpah, placed him in the honorable mention category. And the fast food franchise that sponsored the event gave him a coupon for some french fries.

A few days later Alex drove to the restaurant to get the fries, and on the way home, he looked over at his son, who was quietly munching away. He thought that a bag of fries must have seemed a meager reward to the boy, but, as if reading his father's mind, Cliff looked up and said, "These are the best fries I've ever eaten."

Before we leave this father and son, I want to share this short but powerful conversation, which produced another story.

A few minutes later, Alex gestured out of his window, drawing Cliff's attention to Gus, a familiar figure in the neighborhood, who, when weather allowed, spread used books and magazines on a blanket to sell to passersby. Despite Gus' filthy clothes and advancing senility, his great intelligence was apparent to all in the neighborhood.

CLIFF: (Turning in his seat and watching Gus) I wonder what happened to him.

ALEX: I heard that he has a college degree.

CLIFF: I don't believe that.

ALEX: It's possible. Graduating from college doesn't guarantee success. You also have to have a certain kind of fearlessness. Maybe something frightened him . . . some big opportunity. Maybe he was afraid of trying and just gave up.

CLIFF: Who knows?

ALEX: I know I'm very proud of you. That contest came from out of the blue, but you took the chance.

CLIFF: (He doesn't answer with words, but continues munching his fries, wearing a bit of a grin, and, perhaps, savoring his success.)

From one homework assignment, this father was able to teach his son some valuable lessons about taking risks. Never underestimate the power of a story.

My Story

I was much younger than that young man when I realized how deeply I could be affected by a story. In fact, I was eight and was spending a week at the Woodcraft Rangers camp in a southern California forest. My group was led by a counselor who could tell great ghost stories. One night, as we sat around a camp fire, this counselor handed one of the boys a large, richly detailed, hand-carved box. He told the boy that no matter what happened, to keep it closed and to be sure not to look inside.

As the counselor weaved his tale about an evil warlock who'd lost his head, we boys began to suspect that the skull must be in the very box which this boy clutched tightly in his arms. The counselor warned us that anyone who looked at the head would be changed horrifically, for life. Well, you can probably guess what happened. Just when this counselor felt we were sufficiently frightened out of our wits, he snatched the box from this boy, gave a screech of terror, and threw the box in the air.

Everyone screamed. But no one in that circle was more frightened than I as I fell to the ground, face first, my arms sweeping over my head to protect myself from this ghastly image. What I hadn't realized was that someone had marked the ground beneath us, with white chalk, in an Indian design. So when the imagined horror had ended, I looked up and was greeted by the screams of the other boys. There I was, kneeling in the moonlight, white chalk covering my face. This started a rumor that swept through the camp like wildfire.

Many believed that I had been transformed by the skull—that my face had contorted and turned white. It took me a while to convince the others that it was only a joke, that I was the same old Johnny. The truth, however, is that I wasn't.

Oh, the chalk was quickly dusted off, but I never forgot this man's story, and the power he'd been able to exercise with it.

How I Learned About the Power

As I grew older I realized that I had probably been more deeply affected by his tale than the others, because I had been raised to believe in stories. I'm from a family that shares its history in personal narratives. Since infancy, my sister, Carole, and I had heard them from my mother, my grandmother, and my Aunt Lois—a triumvirate of women powerful enough to tackle the meanest gang roaming the neighborhood, and inspiring enough to send me and my sister, Carole, up and away, to reach for the sky.

My Aunt Lois was, by any standards, a remarkable woman. A child of the Depression, she didn't believe in just staring life in the face; she tackled it, and won. She wasn't related to me by blood. But like many kids raised in an extended family, I had lots of "relatives," that is, people who were good friends and neighbors of my parents, and to whom I was answerable. In other words, they had permission to whack the daylights out of me, if they caught me misbehaving. Believe me, it can help keep a kid on the straight and narrow if he knows that when his feet hit the streets, there are, at any given moment, 20 pairs of eyes trained on his back.

Somewhere along the way, Aunt Lois learned how to talk to us kids so we would listen. One of her first jobs, in fact, was counseling gang members. She eventually began teaching psychology at UCLA, and for three years she was voted the most significant professor by her students. I know now that she had a gift. She would really listen when a kid had a problem, then she'd present the problem back in story form, so you could see it from a different point of view.

I can almost hear her words, so very long ago, talking to me about some problem or other. "Let's look at it this way, John," she'd say. "This teacher has 29 kids in class. I wonder what might have made her so grumpy that day. Maybe it was . . . ," Aunt Lois would continue adding her bits of humor and insight while I listened carefully, then she'd pull me gently back into the problem. "And after all that, when she arrived at school, shook off some of the rain, walked into class, and there you were, not meaning to make things worse for her but . . ."

By the time she finished, Aunt Lois had shown me the other guy's side. The process made her seem non-judgmental. You felt you could tell her anything. What a rich life she and the others provided for me. But several years ago, I came home and found a message on my answering machine that Aunt Lois was in the hospital and might die at any moment. I called the hospital, and the nurse on Aunt Lois' case said, "Come now." They'd given my name to the guard out front, and as soon as I arrived, they rushed me up to her bedside. I saw it was already too late. Her eyes were shut, her breathing was shallow and she only stirred occasionally to gasp for breath. I took her hand. I was in shock.

As I sat there, I began to recall her stories, her battles over adversity. I knew then that though she might be lost to this world, she never would be for me, or for any of the young people who'd been blessed to know her. She had given us a mighty legacy. Her stories had actually defined who she was. Because of them I understood the pattern of her actions, her purposes, designs, and hopes for this world, and knew she would live on.

Putting Stories To Work

One of my first jobs out of undergraduate school was in the late sixties, when I worked as a teacher in the Los Angeles public schools. I'd requested work in the kindergarten. So it came as a surprise when the principal insisted that I teach a sixth grade class. "We need a man in that spot," he said, "to handle some of those tough boys."

He was right about one thing, many of those kids were tough, and came from some of the meanest streets in the city. Still, I was a lot bigger than they and could have easily ruled by intimidation. But I decided something else was in order. I captured their attention with my old standby, stories. I began with ghost tales. (No, I didn't use any boxes as props.) Soon the kids were looking forward to them with such enthusiasm that I could get them to concentrate on even the most challenging subjects, but only if they knew one of my stories was coming at the end of the day. They loved the drama and humor and suspense so much that I don't think they even noticed when I switched from ghost stories to real life dramas—tales that often included lessons learned from my childhood.

After I'd returned to college and earned a master's degree in counseling, I began speaking to adults in groups. Then I decided to try to motivate teenagers. I can still remember my first high school address in 1982. Believe me, nothing is more sobering than speaking to a group of 1,800 teenagers. I stood there looking out at all those kids, squirming and tittering in their seats, quieting only when the principal stood to introduce me. I looked out at their faces, some full of expectation, others staring belligerently, victims of inattentiveness and neglect. In the hush, I could almost hear their hormones raging.

As I walked to center stage, I wondered what I had been thinking to take on an assignment like this. I'm not Eddie Murphy or Michael

Jordan or Bill Cosby. I'm just a regular guy. The only other time I'd addressed kids was in a ninth grade speech class, and I was a kid myself. My assignment was to pretend that I was telling reluctant taxpayers why they should pay their taxes. You can imagine how that ended.

My heart raced as I was introduced. I broke into my prepared material, using all of what I'd rehearsed and memorized. I looked out and saw from the faces that I was on a mild roll. Then, 20 minutes into the presentation, my life passed before me. Not only had I forgotten the point I was trying to make, but I'd run out of material. What was I going to do?

I took a deep breath and did what came naturally. I began telling a story—one about my life. Then I looked at the audience—silence. They were listening. And from that moment on I knew I had made a major transition in my life.

I've since traveled to 30 states, spoken to more than a million teenagers, and about half as many parents. My message is a simple one. I say that everyone's behavior is guided by a story that has recurring themes and residues of the past. I teach them that our stories affect the ways we talk to one another and guide the way we live our lives. What I don't tell them, because time would not allow it, is that these stories we live by are called core stories. But if we, as parents, are to truly understand our teenagers and why we parent as we do, we will have to understand our own core stories and how they may rule us. Let's explore that in our next chapter.

What Teens Say:
"These Are The Issues We Usually Disagree With Our Parents About . . ."

(Each phrase or sentence represents a new voice.)

- "Stepparents."
- "Gang membership."
- "Attending rock concerts."
- "Curfews."
- "Going out."
- "Abortions."
- "Money and how to spend it."
- "Sleeping late."
- "Animal rights."
- "Dating."
- "When I'll be old enough to do things on my own."
- "The telephone."
- "Telephone bills."
- "Riding in a boy's car."
- "My mom's boyfriends."
- "George Bush, Dan Quayle, homelessness, and the environment."
- "That I should have a car."
- "A serious love relationship."
- "Expensive clothes."
- "My career choices."
- "Religion (I have none, they are devout Catholics)."
- "How many extracurricular activities I have."
- "The purpose of life."
- "Racial issues."
- "Interracial dating."
- "Unchaperoned parties."
- "Junk food."
- "Me smoking."
- "Foreign trade."
- "They are backseat drivers when I drive."
- "Dating older men."
- "Me not practicing my instrument."

- "My stepmom and her son."
- "My dreams."
- "The drinking age."
- "Capital punishment."
- "Dances and clothes."
- "Premarital sex."
- "Me wearing black."
- "Judgement of people's character."
- "Sexually transmitted diseases, especially AIDS."
- "What I wear—they don't like pants, shorts, or mini–skirts."
- "Movie ratings."
- "My mom and dad's constant arguing."
- "What to watch on TV."
- "Sex and birth control."
- "Taking a year off before starting college."

4

Core Stories

I'd like to begin here by reintroducing Pat and Lisa. Their experiences, and those of other families you are about to meet, may shed light on hidden motivations that affect the way you communicate with your teenager.

I call these disguised factors core stories. They include the assumptions, stereotypes, and halftruths we've developed about ourselves and people we know. Unfortunately, they are often based upon negative experiences from the past. And like parentisms and lectures, they interfere with good communication.

When Pat discovered Lisa's panties on the couch, for example, her mind leaped ahead to the assumption that Lisa had behaved incautiously. Rather than searching out the truth, Pat read what I call the "Headline News." (EXTRA! EXTRA! READ ALL ABOUT IT! LISA IS SLEEPING WITH HER BOYFRIEND!) The result, of course, is that Pat missed out on an important conversation with her daughter, at a time when the girl most needed her mother's counsel.

Furthermore, Pat not only failed to question Lisa, but even seemed fearful of chastising. So, as you can see, it's vital to examine Pat's hidden motives, that is, her core story. Without this careful look, we'd be left wondering why an intelligent, well-meaning mother, who did not approve of teenage sex, would rush full speed ahead, and begin supplying her daughter with condoms.

When I probed, Pat admitted to me that although she was a virgin when she married, her younger sister, who had become sexually active at 15, discovered she was pregnant and had an illegal, conscience-rending, life-threatening abortion. On a scale weighing life's experiences, that's a pretty heavy incident, especially in light of the fact that Pat and her sister handled all of this in secrecy, never telling their folks about any of it. They believed their parents would throw their unfortunate daughter out of the house.

So while her sister was in physical pain, Pat was suffering psychologically. She said that, at one point during the recuperation, she worried that her sister might actually die from an infection. With that in mind, remember Pat's comment to me after she'd given Lisa (who was also 15) the condoms. "I wish my mother and I had been able to talk like that."

I see a clear connection between that frightened, confused, young Pat who prayed over her sister's bedside, and the Pat who dispenses condoms to her daughter and takes pride in seeming more like a sister than a mother. It enables us to understand how much Pat's sense of disappointment over her own relationship with her parents came between her and her daughter.

Pat and Lisa offer the best demonstration possible of how core stories can haunt us, destroying prime opportunities for communication. Sometimes, our fears are based upon things we've not experienced, but have heard about. We often rush to judge, then assume that the same mishaps will befall our children. In truth, haven't you ever felt this way?

Try recalling your last irrational explosion or seethingly silent conflict with your teenager. How did your core story prevent you from engaging in a heartfelt conversation? The subject doesn't have to concern sex. What about school work? I've found that to be one of the most emotionally charged issues between parents and teenagers.

Lies As Powerful As the Truth

One man in Chicago, whom we shall call Steven, is a multimillionaire who made his fortune in the stock market during the high-rolling eighties. A few years ago, he switched his attention to his son's poor showing at school. In fact, Steven became so immersed in the work of his 16-year-old son that he began setting up weekly conference calls with the young man's teachers.

Each Friday, Steven would sit in his spectacular office, complete with an expansive view of the city, and have his son brought over so they could discuss the week's progress in a conference call. After a few weeks of this, the boy's headmaster appealed to the wife, Karen, to put a stop to it. Not surprisingly, this financial baron was intimidating the teachers. One told the headmaster that he was afraid to give the boy failing grades.

Karen said when her husband refused to back off, she turned to her mother-in-law for advice. Does it surprise you to learn that Steven's mother said her son had failed miserably throughout high school?

That's what his mom said, but when faced with the truth, Steven denied it, said his mother was exaggerating, and that he hadn't really done poorly. He may have believed what he was saying. I suspect he'd wiped the truth right out of his memory. When his mother mailed one of his old report cards to their home—with two Ds and two Fs—he had to admit the truth, but only after his mother warned she had more of the same packed away, and would keep sending them if necessary.

I find Steven's story captivating, particularly because it demonstrates something essential about core stories: A lie can be as powerful as the truth, if you can get someone to believe it.

I don't doubt that Steven loved his son, and didn't mean to mislead him or embarrass him, but he was driven by his core story, and it blocked any genuine communication between him and his son. He told himself and others that he was successful today only because he'd been a virtual whiz kid when in school. Deep down, though, he must have sensed that wasn't true because his past mistakes hammered away at him, closing him off to his son's needs. And as it turned out, his son knew precisely what he needed.

Steven was chastened by the memory of his old report cards, but I can't tell you that he gave up bullying altogether, or that he even admitted that he'd made some mistakes with his son. Unfortunately, none of that occurred. But he did take an important step on the path to communication. He asked his son what he wanted out of life, and he kept his mouth shut while the boy talked.

His son asked for some breathing room, said he didn't know for sure what he wanted to become, that he hoped to one day write some good plays, and have them produced. He said the only thing he was sure of was that he didn't want to be groomed for a career in high finance.

Steven must have heard him. He eventually allowed his son to change schools in fact, to one that was less competitive. The boy's grades didn't surge to the top, but Karen said, "Once he enrolled in a school he really liked, he worked harder."

I wouldn't call it a happy ending yet, but I'd label it as a great start. Delving into core stories can often yield rewards. I'm going to offer some ways for you to identify yours.

Discovering Your Core Stories

Try recalling your most irrational responses to some conflicts you've had with your teenager, particularly those issues that keep resurfacing.

Secondly, after searching your memory file thoroughly, try to connect them to some motivating force. Let me show you a list one woman compiled after a few hours. Yours can evolve over a matter of hours or days as you consider the subject.

CONFLICTS	MY CORE STORIES
Son comes home late from school	I always had to get home right after school to help take care of my little sister and brother. I wasn't allowed to join the debating team. I was on time. My child should be on time.
He doesn't do family chores	My mother was a slob. I was humiliated that she took such terrible care of the house. I always cleaned for her. That's what children do.
His bedroom is sloppy	(See above, maybe the two are related.) I was always neat and clean.
Has been overheard using profanity	I have never spoken like that, except once or twice. I worry that my son will be a filthy-mouthed ruffian like the other kids.
Refuses to participate in church	When I was a kid, everyone knew my parents were failures. If I can't get my son to church it makes me feel like a failure.
He sulks	It makes me feel unappreciated. This could have a connection to the times my husband and I have stopped talking to one another for a few days when we're angry. This is the same thing my parents did when they were angry with one another, especially my mom, when Daddy drank.

I'm not suggesting for a minute that it's your fault when your youngster is uncooperative. But if you have core issues connected to these behavior patterns, you may lose control when the conflict arises, and find yourself unable to communicate effectively. Understanding why you fly off the handle may help you retain control so you can talk it out and find a solution. Ask yourself, "what makes this such an issue for me? What is my story?"

Once you've identified them, be particularly cautious about those core stories that may force you to set your teenager up for a conflict. Let me give you an example.

One woman I worked with had a 14-year-old daughter who loved attending the Friday evening dances at her junior high each month. When this girl moved on to her freshman year, her grades began to slip. The mother threatened that if she didn't "buckle down" and work harder, she wouldn't let her attend the next dance. Two nights before a mid-term exam, the mother had to go out for an appointment, and told her daughter, "If I come home and find that you haven't been studying, the dance is off."

When the mother returned, she discovered her daughter hadn't picked up a book. In fact, according to an older brother, she kept the telephone tied up for most of the evening. Her mother blew up, and for such direct defiance, she tripled the punishment, telling her daughter she couldn't go to the next three dances. She said she kept asking her daughter, "Why did you do this? Why are you screwing up your life?" Her daughter's only answer was, "I don't know."

I don't find it surprising that the girl didn't have an answer. It's obvious that something else was going on beneath the surface. Later, the woman confided in me that she felt terrible about having screamed, and believed that she'd gone overboard with the punishment. Well, while I certainly don't condone the girl's behavior, and believe it was necessary for her mother to respond forcefully, I couldn't help but feel there was a core story connected to this. As it turned out, it wasn't at all difficult to find.

When I asked the mother why she had chosen this particular form of punishment, she shrugged and explained that, at the time, the dances seemed like the greatest incentives for better grades. Then I asked her to recall her own experiences at school dances. She didn't have to think long about that. She said that as a teenager, she'd never attended a school dance. Her parents considered dancing a sin. In order to get along with her parents, she pretended she didn't want to go. But she grieved over each missed affair.

"And what about you, now that you're a mother?" I asked. "What do you think about your daughter attending these dances?"

Once again, she wasted no time before speaking. "They're a joy for my daughter. You wouldn't believe how long she takes getting ready for them. I love seeing her like that. And when she comes home her face is glowing."

"But what about lately?" I asked. "Do you really believe you got the results you wanted?"

This time, before she spoke, she wiped her mouth with her hand, as if encouraging herself to say words that were fresh and clean, and which signaled a break from her past. "I've made those dances the same occasions for misery that my parents turned them into for me," she said sadly.

I told her I agreed and added that "I also think you've set your daughter up. She was angry about it but instead of telling you, because she didn't understand anymore than you did what was occurring, she picked up the phone and chattered away, defying your orders."

I told her that the next time, rather than threatening her daughter with punishments, she might instead consider setting up consequences. I explained that threats and ultimatums are like dares to teenagers; they often find them thrilling to defy. A consequence though, is a logical response, and because it won't have a connection to your core story, it is a hand that can be dealt without hysteria.

A teenager, for instance, might spend a week's worth of lunch money on a movie ticket. What's the logical consequence? He can go without lunch for a week. (It really won't kill him, I promise.) Now, let's say this woman's daughter fails a test because she spends too much time on the phone. The consequence? No phone calls until the grade improves.

Later in this book, I'll go into detail about how to set up consequences. You'll find they can help you avoid getting ensnared in your core stories, allowing you and your teenager to really communicate.

Learning Teens' Hidden Assumptions

First, however, I'd like to examine the flip side of core stories, because they aren't limited to adults. Good communication is a two-way street, requiring that our youngsters also be made aware of their false assumptions and stereotypes. The young people we've discussed in this chapter had stories of their own which threw up roadblocks.

Lisa thought her mother was encouraging her to do something she didn't want to do. She completely misread the pain her mother was feeling. Like so many of her contemporaries, she felt grown-ups really didn't care. Steven's son, who was being groomed to be a financial baron, didn't tell his parents he'd rather write plays, because he assumed they wouldn't care or listen. The girl who was missing the school dances, and may have sensed that her mother was envious of her carefree lifestyle, began to behave out of character.

There's a big difference, though, when it comes to dealing with a teenager's mis-assumptions. He can't be expected to analyze his motivations in a sophisticated manner. As the adult in the relationship, you must lead the way. Your youngster will learn by watching you deal with your issues. If you begin facing up to your old core stories, you will encourage your youngster to understand his, and to end years of noncommunication.

Begin by telling your youngster your story, and why certain issues have been emotional dynamite within you. This may be one of the most difficult steps you take. But when parents reveal their own inner struggles it helps break down a young person's defenses and opens the way for him to share his secret fears and beliefs. It allows us to see and hear our youngster and to demonstrate that we share his concerns. The best time to do this is when the youth is "off-guard." Plan ahead, but don't make an appointment to talk—as you would when a specific issue is involved. Choose a casual time, after some leisure activity or during shared work time. Be honest and allow your child to comment.

Unfortunately, if you don't tell your child the truth and offer him vital alternatives which he can live by, someone else may come along with his or her persuasive stories and capture your child's mind. Or just as frightening, your child may create his own story about himself, based upon the negative impressions he holds of himself.

The Power of Commitment

The next obvious task then, is learning to rewrite a core story. I know a woman who changed the course of her sister's life by changing her core story. Let me tell you about these women.

These two sisters were raised 30 years ago, in an upper middle-class neighborhood in Brooklyn, New York. Their mother, a widow, was one of the few successful business women in those days. She was a caring and loving parent when she was home, but unfortunately her work forced her to spend a great deal of time in the office, away from her daughters. For that reason, the older girl, Joyce, began to serve as an unofficial surrogate to Lee, two years her junior.

Joyce, the older sister, was a stellar student, and began reading and writing long before most children her age. By the time she was in the ninth grade, she'd earned a reputation as a young scholar. Teachers at the local junior high were expecting more of the same from Lee when she entered the school.

But she soon disappointed them all. Although she'd gotten through elementary school with satisfactory grades, junior high school, with its quickly moving schedule and heavier academic load, seemed to throw the girl off balance. Lee's teachers said she had trouble following directions, understanding the simplest classes, and she quickly fell behind. Her grades were so poor that she was barely promoted each year, and by the time she reached high school, she was thinking of dropping out.

When their mother intervened on the younger girl's behalf, a guidance counselor offered this advice. "Don't worry about her bad grades. In the end they won't matter. She has trouble with the cognitive process; she just can't think fast enough. You should encourage her to become a domestic or a file clerk. Don't expect anything more."

The mother was wise enough to transfer the girl to a smaller school, where classes might be easier, and where, of course, they could escape this dreadful guidance counselor. But it was to no avail. By then, Lee had started keeping the company of other girls who were doing poorly in school. One had spent time in a reformatory for stealing and Lee seemed to be doomed to follow in her footsteps. One afternoon, when she was supposed to be in class, she was caught stealing a handkerchief at a local five and dime. Fortunately, the store manager had taken pity on her and not called the police.

At this point, Joyce decided to take matters into her own hands. In college by now, with a part-time job, she had little time to spare, but she made time to be with her sister. Joyce told Lee that she understood her. She told her she was convinced she was a genius, and that many people like her had also been misunderstood in school. She told Lee that she could do anything she wanted to in life, that she had a special gift from God, and that she just had to begin learning more, before it was too late and her brain cells got rusty.

They spent long afternoons at the public library, making several trips a month. The librarian came to know them on a first name basis. Joyce helped Lee select some of the great works of literature, and they began to discuss them together. In fact, during the summer of 1962, Joyce gave her sister an unusual assignment. She challenged her to read Tolstoy's *War and Peace*, and to write a lengthy paper on it.

When it was finished, Joyce praised her sister's work. She even took the paper to a college professor and asked him to write encouraging comments in the margins. This was a heady experience for Lee, who was only 16 years old. From there, Joyce selected several more books for her sister, including "The Complete Works of Sigmund Freud," and a series of books by Ayn Rand. When Lee had completed the works by Rand, Joyce enrolled her sister in a college course designed to examine Rand's philosophy.

The next step in Joyce's plan also worked. She convinced Lee, who had dropped out of high school the year before, to go to night school and earn a diploma. Lee did and eventually enrolled in a small college. I'm glad to say that's not the end of the story. She struggled through her college courses, but did graduate. She became a writer and began winning awards for her work. In fact, I'm sure if I were to give you her real name, you'd recognize it immediately.

But there's more. It wasn't until four years ago that Lee discovered it hadn't been laziness or stupidity that had held her back in junior high and high school. She was diagnosed as having a severe learning disability. She has an auditory processing problem. She has always been able to read well, but she had difficulty taking in and comprehending a large body of information, such as when listening to a lecture.

Once her problem was given a name, Lee developed even more self-confidence. She realized that she simply learns things differently. She developed a desire to understand all the things she'd been afraid to tackle. She asked a friend to tell her how to read a map. But rather than just listening, she recorded his words, wrote them down, then broke the information into smaller categories. For the first time in her life, she was able to read a map and stopped getting lost in the small town she had moved to with her family. She then tackled geography, math, and science.

I would love to have introduced you to Joyce today, to get some feedback from her about what she did with her sister, how she sized up the core story of this 16-year-old discouraged and lost girl, who seemed to have "trouble with cognitive process," and how she turned her sister's life around. But I cannot talk to Joyce, she died at a young age. But I'm certain that if she could see her sister now, she would know that she made a real contribution to this earth. Her love, concern, and belief in her sister is born again with every story that Lee writes, every person her stories inspire.

What Joyce did for her sister is what so many of us must decide to do for our children. We can virtually save their lives. First, though, we must rewrite our own stories which limit the way we see our children.

Rewriting a Core Story

Following is a course of action that can help you rewrite your core story:

1. Take a brutally honest look at the kind of character traits you believe your teenager possesses. Do you believe he'll never "make anything of himself," for instance, or that his poor showing at school means he'll never have a chance to succeed. Do you believe he's lazy? Lacks gumption? Is dishonest?

   If it's an opinion you'd like to change, walk backwards mentally and trace the origins of your beliefs. Ask yourself what might have occurred to make you believe this about your child. Once again, you needn't search for some major event.

   Developing a negative opinion about someone can happen quite suddenly. No one proved this better than the director Alfred Hitchcock in "Dial M for Murder." In this 1955 movie, viewers were introduced to three key players: the elegant Grace Kelly, a trusting wife; Robert Cummings, who played her former lover; and Ray Milland, her charming and affable husband. Right from the start, thanks to the movie's title, we viewers knew that one character would soon be up to no good. It wasn't long before we suspected the Milland character on the basis of one telephone conversation.

   We watched as Milland told the person on the other end of the line that he was unable to leave his apartment because he had suffered a minor leg injury. Well, we had just seen him moving about quite nicely, so it was apparent he was not telling the truth. It was only a fib, of course, something said to avoid an inconvenience. But none of us were fools. That one lie was enough to convince every viewer that if a murder was going to be committed, the Milland character would have his evil hand in it.

The truth is, most of us begin viewing our teenagers in the same manner as Hitchcock's audience. We know teenagers can get into trouble, cause terrible calamities, and twist our hearts if they turn on us. But because we love them, we want to trust them. We sit back and observe with the greatest of expectations. But each time our children fail us, be it disappointing grades, a lie here or there, a confrontation, a show of dishonesty or disrespect, we feel as if they are hammering away at us. Bit by bit, despite our love, our expectations, our great sacrifices, we begin to doubt our children, begin writing stories about them and who they will become.

Ask yourself when you stopped writing off unpleasant incidents as mere childish pranks and began thinking that your teenager had character flaws. Take time, now that you are in a more reflective mode, to reconsider the circumstances preceding your child's "behavior problem." Had you just moved to a new neighborhood, perhaps? Just divorced? Remarried? Were you arguing a great deal with your spouse? Were you going through a difficult time at work? These aren't excuses for your child, just the facts that may help you face your disappointments as well as understand them.

2. This next exercise is designed to help you understand your role as a parent: Try to visualize your teenager as someone crossing a long and narrow bridge that leads to maturity. Picture her first crawling, then struggling to stand. With each step, you can see her growing older and more surefooted. But just as she begins to look more like an adult, the winds of life pick up and begin blowing furiously, sometimes rocking the flimsy bridge.

You are in a prime position to observe her, because you know her and the path so well. You can almost predict when and where she will stumble. She grabs for the ropes and she is almost pitched over the sides. But you cannot give her a hand. Her journey must be solo. Your added weight on this bridge might destroy you both.

What you can do, however, is guide her across with your words, with your steady and reassuring manner. You must remain faithful and steadfast, watching her progress from the other side. You know she may slip and fall and, perhaps, disappoint you, as well as herself. But take comfort, she'll continue to progress, no matter how small her steps.

When you see her slipping again, try to refrain from shouting out recklessly; it might be her undoing. Remember that your words may buffer her from the fierce wind, but your teenager can still feel it, and may continue to slip. It is important for you to remain confident, encouraging with words and body language. With your help, she will cross over.

3. The next exercise is designed to help you forgive your teenager for past mistakes. The truth is, he may have earned your distrust. Go into a room where you can be alone and set up two chairs. In one, you may want to place a pillow or some item that you associate with your child. Maybe even a keepsake such as an old lunchbox or doll. Sit facing that chair and pretend you're having a conversation with your teenager.

Tell him (the chair, that is) what you're disappointed or angry about. What is it specifically that he did or didn't do? Say aloud:

"I expected you to (fill in the blanks) . . ."

"Instead, you did. . . ."

"When you did that you. . . . to me."

"But because you are human and are subject to failure I release you from my expectations."

Picture yourself here letting go. See your hands slipping gently away from his shoulders or hand. Remember you can only guide your youngster across that bridge with your words, with your encouraging actions and body language. Release him of your expectations.

Continue your list of grievances and repeat this exercise as many times as is necessary so you can begin a new relationship with your teenager. Don't be afraid to cry. Some parents feel ashamed if they cry over a child's misbehavior but the truth is that you can be wounded by it. Who else would we love so unconditionally? Who else would we sacrifice so much for? Your tears may be a part of your forgiveness process. Let them wash away your anger and disappointments.

4. Unburdened by grievances from the past, begin to consider your child's dreams. Remember that as human beings our greatest gift is that we have the ability to dream. Does your child have wild and impossible goals? Impractical ambitions? Is he looking forward to being an adult? Making plans for the future? Congratulate yourself. Dreaming is healthy for hearts and minds.

When your teenager last shared his dreams with you, did you, through body language or words, discourage him? When he last told you of his hopes to be a poet, athlete, singer, etc., did you patronize him, speak sarcastically, or ignore him? If you reacted negatively you need to know why. Take a look at any core issues you might have that are connected to the subject. Did your parents treat you in much the same way? Were you discouraged from dreaming, told to be more practical, more realistic? Try to separate your issues from your teenager's goals.

5. Initiate a new conversation with your child about his goals. Invite him to a coffee shop or out for a walk, someplace where you won't be distracted. Ask him, if he appears cautious, what he would be if he could do anything. Assure your child that while you will be there to remind him of life's responsibilities ("You'll need a skill to help pay your bills") you also want to give him the emotional support he needs to fulfill that dream.

   This is a good time to share a story with him about someone who either discouraged or helped you. Or you can tell him a story about what you did or didn't get to try out for.

6. Dream together. Draw mental pictures aloud of your child fulfilling his goals. ("I'm going to remember that practical joke you pulled last week and when *Time Magazine* votes you 'Man of the Year,' I can tell the reporter all about it.")

   As the weeks pass you might want to recommend some books and articles, or a movie or television show concerning the subject. You'll show him that you've taken him seriously. You'll be surprised at how much you two will have to talk about.

7. Keep an open mind and *really* listen when your teenager talks about plans for college or professional school. Forcing someone to go to college is akin to stepping on that bridge and trying to drag your child across. You might reach the other side but you won't be happy with the results.

   If college is part of your child's plans, offer to become a part of the process in selecting and visiting institutions. Several books and services are now available that can help you both find schools that meet your youngster's academic, financial, and emotional needs.

   Most importantly, remember that, at this point, your teenager's core story may *seem* irreversible. He may seem ill-mannered and without positive goals, but remember, if a young college girl had the determination to turn her sister's life around, you, as a mature adult and caring parent, can certainly make the same effort. You'll need some genuine stories to get this new relationship going. And in our next chapter we'll learn how to present real truths about our pasts to our youngsters—not idealized versions.

BIG BANGS
What Teens Say:
"The Worst Confrontation With
My Parents Was . . ."

(Each new sentence or phrase represents a voice.)

- "Every time grades come out."
- "When my mom made me see my dad."
- "When I shoplifted (once)."
- "When I got caught drinking."
- "When I lost complete control and said, 'F#!* you!' to my father."
- "When they accused me of having sex and taking drugs."
- "When I wanted my parents to get a divorce."
- "When I wrecked the car."
- "When I got caught with marijuana in the eighth grade."
- "When I lost my jacket."
- "When I had to choose which parent I'd live with."
- "When I found out something about my dad that he didn't want me to know."
- "When my brother had a drinking party in my dad's motel room and I attended (for 10 minutes)."
- "When my mom tried to put my head through the windshield."
- "When I defended my sister because she was dating a black guy."
- "When I took the car and didn't have a license."
- "When I sneaked out after bedtime."
- "When I came home a half-hour late."
- "When I got a speeding ticket—32 miles over the limit."
- "Over a $900 phone bill."
- "Because my father is a bigot."
- "When I skipped Christmas dinner."
- "When I spent the night with a guy when I was in the tenth grade."
- "When my folks accused me of losing the family history books (then they found them three months later)."
- "Over which colleges I should apply to."
- "When my mother found a pack of cigarettes in my drawer."

- "When my dad threw something at me."
- "When my parents talked about getting a divorce on my sister's birthday and I was so angry I left for the night."
- "When they went away for the weekend and I had a party."
- "When I stuck up for my mom."
- "Too numerous to mention."
- "When I called my mom a pig."
- "When my mom told me we were moving after the ninth grade."
- "Over anything related to sex."
- "Over religion and what they want me to believe."
- "When my sister got pregnant."
- "When my mom thought I was pregnant—I wasn't."
- "When I fought my cousin in public."
- "When my parents didn't like my best friend."
- "When my aunt hit me and I hit her back, and then I tried to burn the house down."
- "When a C appeared on my report card."
- "When I was suspended the first time."
- "When I came home drunk."
- "When I stole money from them."
- "When I was sneaking out and the police department called my mom and she came out and saw me and just stood in the hallway and stared at me, so I felt awful."
- "When my dad hit me."
- "When I wished out loud my dog was dead so I didn't have to walk him, and my dad got angry."
- "When I dented my aunt's car."
- "When I almost moved in with my father."
- "When they found alcohol in my room."
- "When I was ten hours late."
- "When I felt too sick to put away the dishes and my dad threw my clothes down the hall, so I ran away."
- "When my stepmom treated me like crap."
- "When I tried to commit suicide."
- "When they found a letter I wrote to my friends that had a lot of bad words in it."
- "When I stayed out until 2 a.m. and my mom was crying when I showed up."
- "Over which major in college they wanted me to choose."
- "When my mom told me to go to hell."

- "When my parents separated."
- "When my brother hit me in the stomach with a baseball bat and my parents defended him, and I ruined my door and wall and beat up my mom and ran away."
- "When I sneaked out last New Year's Eve and then no one would drive me home so I had to call my parents at six in the morning."

II

NEW
BEGINNINGS

5

Dismantling
The Berlin Walls
In Our Homes

If you've seen the movie "Vice Versa," you laughed along with millions of viewers as a seventh grader, played by Fred Savage of ABC's "Wonder Years," switched bodies with his father, a harried executive, played by Judge Reinhold. This magical transposition produced an adult body with a teenager's brain and personality, and vice versa. That meant the twelve-year-old "father" had to go to school instead of the office.

Just before his father left for class, the son tried to prepare dad for the brave new world he was entering. "It's been a long while since you went to school, Dad."

"What do you mean?" the father asked naively.

"It's not like 'Happy Days' anymore," continued the son. "All I'm saying is be careful out there."

It didn't take the father long to understand why his son was worried about him. One after another, the principal, hockey coach, homeroom teacher, and the school bully took turns humiliating, threatening, abusing him and discouraging him from his dreams.

In the end, the father admitted that being a teenager today is hard work. When they were finally back to normal, the two were shown genuinely talking and listening to each other. It's a great fantasy, but there is a realistic hope for generations to communicate. It's up to the adults to find more practical approaches for spanning the generations. Let's start by pulling back from the situation and taking a bird's eye view at what so many families are doing. It may help you understand why it sometimes feels that although you share the same home with your teenager, when it comes to communication, it's as if you're separated by a mighty wall.

Here you are on one side, working busily, trying to give your youngster the comforts of life that you may never have had. In fact, you wouldn't do half this much for anyone else. Occasionally, you look over at your teenager and think, "If only I'd had these advantages!" and, "What a great life this kid has." But to our teenagers, life is no bed of roses. Parents and teachers are pressuring them to move in one direction and their peers in another. Our kids wonder why we don't understand just how tough it is for them. Adults want to protect kids, keep them safe, and prepare them for the future. Kids want to explore, take chances, and discover their own boundaries and live for today.

How We Built Those Walls

Given these opposing purposes and world views, we often erect invisible walls, so we can survive adolescence under the same roof. These walls are our own secrets, unexpressed feelings, swallowed apologies, the tiny hidden truths, and the big ones, too, from our pasts and present-day dilemmas. Simply put, we've clammed up to co-exist. The greatest problem is that the walls have grown so high, we must literally shout to be heard.

The good news is that the wall in your home can be dismantled. As you begin sharing your narratives with your teenager, you'll find that more may be unearthed than even you're prepared for. In the beginning, you'll have to speak with some caution. Some stories are inappropriate. One man, for instance, told me he was cringing at the dinner table, when his wife began telling their 17-year-old son, who'd just gotten his driver's license, about the drag races she'd been in when growing up in Oregon.

"It was one of the first times in weeks that she'd gotten his attention," the man said. "She didn't realize, until I began making faces at the other end of the table, that this might not be the best story for him to hear."

I can sympathize with the wife's dilemma. When you begin sharing your personal narratives with your teenager and suddenly get a reaction, it is exhilarating. Sometimes you can get so caught up in your own idealized version of yourself as daring, wise, brilliant, and so forth, you can easily find yourself traveling down the wrong road.

For example, take the man whose daughter had been disciplined for cutting classes. He told his daughter that when he was her age, he'd been cited for the same infraction. But he lived to regret his candor. The girl was caught skipping class again, and this time she screamed back at her father, "You did the same thing when you were a kid." Both are cases of parental miscalculations. Still, it's better to take a chance and make that occasional mistake, and in the process create an environment where conversation flows freely, rather than withhold important truths from youngsters. Start being open and above board with your teenager, and you will learn instinctively what to share and what to lock away.

Consider the story of one of my colleagues, Eva, who was raised by her mother, a discouraged woman, whose husband had walked out on her and taken up with his mistress. As my colleague grew up, she wanted very much to contact her father, to know him, spend time with him. But her mother resisted, saying it was obvious from the way he'd walked out on them that he didn't care.

My friend was eventually convinced that her mother was right and gave up. Years later, she met her father at a family wedding. They shook hands and exchanged pleasantries, but nothing more. She never really knew him and he died a few years after they'd been introduced. Eva did quite well in her career, but her personal life was in shambles. She married twice, divorced twice, and all her love relationships ended acrimoniously. She said she had difficulty trusting men. After her mother died, she went back to the old house and was going through a stack of correspondence when she happened upon a letter, written more than 30 years before. It was from her father to her mother.

He begged to be allowed to see Eva. He said he loved the child and missed her terribly, but wrote, "I will honor your request not to visit or contact her. Please let me know how she's doing. Could I call occasionally to say hello?" On and on the letter continued. It seemed he'd written before but the mother had convinced him, too, that a father-daughter relationship was undesirable.

Eva carried the letter outside and sat on the steps, hugging her legs, crying over the love she'd been denied. She tried to see it from her mother's point of view. After all, their lives had been changed by the husband's desertion, at a time when behavior such as his created public scandals. Her mother had probably thought she was protecting her daughter from further harm.

Sitting there, Eva realized she'd never known how it felt to be treasured by a man, to feel secure in his love. How different might her relationships have been, she wondered, if she had experienced her father's love. Today, she says she's not bitter over her mother's deception, that even finding the letter was a gift. But I couldn't help thinking that if her mother had shared the truth with her, it might have been a glorious gift.

How deceptively easy it is for parents to justify keeping secrets. We concoct all kinds of excuses, most of them falling into one of four categories. Let me share these excuses with you, along with some of the secrets adults have created around them. You may well find your own personal mysteries buried among the ruins.

Four Parental Excuses

EXCUSE NUMBER ONE: "I must protect my child. This is too painful for him to hear, he couldn't handle it."

Carole, a southern California physician, felt she could discuss anything with her children, especially with her oldest son George, who at 15 was quite mature. Then she was diagnosed as having breast cancer, and she couldn't bring herself to communicate her own fears to him.

Looking back at the situation now, she said it had to be obvious to George that something terrible was occurring. The minister sometimes visited late at night, and some mornings she would come downstairs with her eyes red from crying. When her parents moved in for an extended visit, George began to question her.

"He asked me what was wrong," Carole said. "What could I say? I thought I might die and I wasn't prepared to tell him that."

Instead, she said nothing, until sometime later, after treatment and a good prognosis. When she told him what had occurred, "he was angry and disappointed in me," she said. "I'd tried to protect him but I'd hurt him a lot."

It caused a temporary rift between them. In fact, the next spring her son asked permission to attend an out-of-state boarding school. She and her husband consented. After graduation, the boy selected a college that was also in another state. Although they saw one another as often as their schedules allowed, Carole said she had only recently felt the closeness between her and George starting to return.

Surely, none of us can blame this woman for her need to simply close in around herself at a time when she might lose her very life. But she shared that story with us to remind other parents of the importance of keeping channels of communication open.

EXCUSE NUMBER TWO: "My child will lose respect for me or stop loving me."

This reminds me of an uncle and his nephew in Connecticut, and their troubling story. This uncle, whom I shall call Howard, was a bachelor who lived near his brother, sister-in-law, and their son, Leif. Howard spent a lot of time with this family and became like a second father to his nephew. As the boy grew up, Howard often went along with the family to circuses, sporting events, movies, and shared holidays with them.

When Leif became a teenager and had conflicts with his parents, there was always his wonderful and brilliant uncle to turn to for heartfelt conversations. But the one subject Howard couldn't share with the boy was the most important. As the years had passed, Howard had come to terms with his own homosexuality. He did confide in his brother and sister-in-law, and they suggested he tell the boy who, by this time, was a junior in high school. But Howard could not.

"It seemed like an impossible subject between us," Howard said. "Like a lot of kids at his school, my nephew had grown virulently homophobic. We'd go out and he'd crack fag jokes." Sometimes, sitting there, listening to his nephew, Howard would play the liberal and defend homosexuals. But that's as far as he went. He was afraid if he admitted the truth about his life, he'd lose his nephew's respect and love.

"I never had the courage to tell him the truth." Howard eventually moved across the country and began a solid and trusting relationship with another man. A few years later, Leif graduated from high school, and following in his favorite uncle's footsteps, he joined the Marines. He wrote to his uncle saying he wanted to visit him before he began his basic training.

"I knew he had to be told," Howard said. "I asked my brother to do it for me." His nephew was reportedly shaken by this news his uncle had kept from him over the years. "He broke down in tears," Howard said.

In the end, the young man decided not to visit and refused to do so for years. "I felt very guilty," Howard said.

EXCUSE NUMBER THREE: "I can't admit that I feel that way. He'll think I'm crazy."

That's probably just how Yvonne, a single parent from North Carolina, was feeling last year after she'd treated her 13-year-old son to a week's stay in a family resort on a Caribbean island. They'd only been there a few hours, when her son made friends with some of the other teenage guests, and decided to spend the evening with them. About midnight, Yvonne walked out to the patio, where she and her son had arranged to meet, but he wasn't there. She had specifically told him not to go down to the beach, but after searching for him for a while, that was where she found him.

"I'm afraid I lost it," Yvonne said. "I started screaming at him in front of his new friends and made him get up and go back to the room with me."

It wasn't long before her anger subsided and Yvonne was sorry for having embarrassed her boy. "What I was really feeling was anger that I'd saved my money to take him down there and he decided he'd rather spend the evening with some kids he'd just met."

She didn't tell him about her feelings of jealousy or loneliness. The incident colored their week's stay and the anger was unresolved.

EXCUSE NUMBER FOUR: "If I tell her what I did she might follow in my footsteps."

There's no better illustration of this than the mother I met from Silver Spring, Maryland who moved to this country from South America. When we met, Claudia was married with two teenage daughters, and for years, she'd kept part of her past secret from them. At 17, she'd had a baby out of wedlock, and her mother had convinced one of their relatives to adopt the child. After her baby girl was born, Claudia was sent to the states to start a new life, and she did. Marrying "well" and raising her two American daughters with love and firmness, she was content.

Two decades later, however, a revolution in Claudia's native country made it impossible for the family who'd adopted her firstborn to continue raising her. They wrote to her in the states, told her of their unfortunate circumstances, and asked if they could send her daughter to her. The political situation was extreme, they added, and they could no longer guarantee the girl's safety.

What was she to do? She'd raised her girls in the strictest moral fashion. She feared that by telling them the truth, they might repeat her mistake. She turned to her priest for guidance. He told her that it was always best to tell the truth. She agreed and sat her daughters down and tearfully told them of her mistake and begged their forgiveness for having lived a lie. She pulled out a baby bootie. It was all she had of their sister, she said. She'd brought it over with her to the states. Although it had been packed away, thoughts of the daughter she had left behind remained. Many nights she'd weep over this infant whom she kissed but once.

The girls listened quietly, then one of them spoke up. "We've always known about her, Mama," she said. Claudia was shocked. "How did you know?"

"I don't know," the girl answered, "we've always known something in your past made you very sad, and we figured it was a child."

It is not surprising that the girls knew. As you'll recall, the young man whose mother had breast cancer also knew there was something wrong. Remember that just as we are the audiences in our children's lives, they are ours. They are with us from the first day of their lives, and they watch and study us as we move through the drama of life. In fact, they come to know us so well that there are few secrets we can keep from them entirely. If you look back over these peoples' actual stories, that illustrate the excuses, there is one striking similarity. No one was helped by keeping the secrets, but everyone was hurt by them.

The reality is that when we refuse to give our children the gift of truth, we do so out of fear of tarnishing our own images or allowing our teenagers to hurt our feelings, and not to protect our youngsters. Covering up the truth not only forces us to hide some of the major details of our past, and withhold lessons learned from our experiences, but it forces us to continue building those walls of secrecy and deceit in our homes.

Of course, it is appropriate to withhold some unnecessary, unrequested information—drag racing stories and cutting class included—but when your child asks for the truth or when a situation occurs that requires it, offer it, for it is truly a gift. Truth is not merely an act of generosity on your part, it's your only defense against that great wall.

Keys to Honest Communication

There are ways to handle uncomfortable conversations so that they 1) draw you and your youngster closer together, and 2) offer your child something to think about.

You'll accomplish both goals by recalling that:

- Your greatest ally is time—time to consider what you will say and how you will say it.
- It is best to begin by admitting your feelings: "It makes me really uncomfortable to tell you this because . . ."
- You can frame your answer through a story. It will help you move the details along to your conclusion: "My point in telling you this is. . . ."
- You can look back on the situation with hindsight and share what you've learned with your youngster, or explain how you've been impacted by the experience.
- Encourage your teenager to respond: "So, how are you feeling about what I've told you?"
- Teach yourself openness and flexibility. If your story moves into unchartered territory, don't panic. You're the same adult who survived countless diaper changes, childhood diseases, sleepless nights, the terrible twos, and even the start of junior high. You can survive this challenge also.

One woman, from upstate New York, was certainly caught off guard when she thought she had reached the end of a story she'd just shared with her 16-year-old son about being offered cocaine at a college party. Her son watched her closely, then said, "Okay, you said no to the cocaine. That's addictive. But did anyone ever offer you a joint?"

"Yes," she admitted, "but I said no."

"But didn't you want it?" he asked.

"I was really curious," she answered.

"You wanted it, right, Mom?"

"I suppose I did, but I still didn't take it."

Then came the question she'd never even asked herself. "But how would it have made a difference?" he asked. "None of those kids you were with got caught, did they? They all finished school and they're probably telling their kids the same thing."

She knew her answer would be important to him, so before speaking, she stalled for time. Here's what she ultimately said:

"Let me make sure I understand what you're asking." She paused, as if considering his question, then lifted her head. "You want to know why it would have made a difference in the long-run. Is that right?"

He nodded affirmativelyand kept watching her face. She paused again, then said, "I want to back up for a minute before I answer you. Your question isn't easy to answer. It frightens me a little, so I'm going to sneak up on it and go through the back door to get to it." She paused again, then began speaking.

"My mother told me that when I was born none of the mothers that she knew breast fed their babies. They were told back then that liquid formulas were just as good as mother's milk. But by the time I had you, we knew differently. The subject had been thoroughly researched and we were told about all the benefits of nursing.

"When it comes to research and information, it's the same thing about marijuana," she continued. "When I was in college, everyone was saying it was harmless. But 20 years later, researchers are telling us that's not true. Oh, it's true that we aren't given as many warnings about marijuana as cocaine or any of the other drugs, but even the little we know about it now is scary. It can cause long-term brain damage. And who knows what they're going to dig up in the next couple of years about the impact of even occasional use?

"So I suppose," she continued, "if I want to answer your question, I'd have to first admit that I did want to try that marijuana. Sure I did. I was curious. And I didn't like letting my friends down. But I'm so glad I didn't try it. Because maybe just one of my friends who did is keeping a close eye on that research and is wondering what researchers are going to discover next about marijuana. Maybe he's scared and is wondering how much of his brain power or what other organ in his body he might have put in jeopardy for those joints."

"I hadn't thought of it that way," her son said.

"I hadn't either," the mother answered, and she left it at that.

Kids Keeping Secrets

If a parent can find the courage to open up to a teenager, as this quick thinking mother did, she's bound to set an important tone in her household. It's as good as hanging a sign over the front door that reads, "There are no invisible walls between the occupants of this house. This is a safe place. Anything can be discussed here." Unfortunately, I meet too many youngsters who are afraid to talk over even the simplest problems with parents. And I've found that one of the surest ways to get a roomful of teenagers laughing is to ask them what subjects they can't discuss with their parents. Their uneasy chortling usually indicates that, in their homes, sensitive issues are taboo.

That's too bad. When I think about what kids discuss with me in private, I can't help but imagine how much better the problems might have been handled if they had turned to their parents.

One ninth grader in Ohio, Cameron, was distressed over his body odor. He said by early morning, despite a rigorous shower, he'd begin sweating in class. His parents probably could have explained to him that this isn't unusual for an adolescent, and they might have helped him come up with a simple solution. But he didn't tell them, and instead, tried to treat his problem clandestinely, using everything from his father's "manly" deodorant to his sister's perfumed powder.

None of that seemed to help though, and to add to his embarrassment, this young man returned to his locker one day to find a shoe box filled with deodorant and soaps. Someone had attached a note to the box saying his "friends" had taken up a donation for him. It ended with the words "You stink."

Why did he keep his problem from his parents? "They tease too much," he said. "If I'd told them it would have been worse."

Then there was Eileen, the eleventh grader from Arizona, who suffered for a year as an old family friend, who was also the family minister, flirted ever so quietly with her. Sometimes, she said, when they were all seated at the dinner table, he'd catch her eye when no one else was looking, and run his tongue over his lips. When she'd remove the dishes from the table, he'd let his hand brush against her thigh. He would suggest a family prayer circle and squeeze her hand and run his thumb across her palm. Once, during a church softball game, she fell and he ran to her aid, lifting her off the ground and rubbing his body against hers.

She asked him to stop several times, but he always feigned innocence. It only ended when she threatened to tell his wife. Why did she keep this secret from her parents? She shrugged her shoulders when I asked. "They wouldn't have believed me," she said.

Finally, there's one story which is especially evocative of our times. In New York, a 15-year-old girl, whom I shall refer to as Rosalind, was sneaking food from her refrigerator to help feed a classmate who, along with her family, was homeless. The classmate begged Rosalind not to tell anyone and said if the authorities knew that she and her family lived in an abandoned building, she'd be sent to a foster home. Rosalind began to steal money and clothes from her parents and when they caught her they accused her of being on drugs. She admitted to that, rather than tell them the truth, because she had promised her friend she'd protect her.

Unfortunately, I never met Rosalind so I wasn't able to ask her why she felt she couldn't have confided in her parents. It's obvious she didn't trust them. How unfortunate. For teenagers, the world can be ugly and compassionless, without adults who will listen to, trust, and believe them.

Novel Narratives

The best way to assure a teenager that you're trustworthy is to learn to discuss difficult subjects with sensitivity. Your teenagers will give you plenty of practice in this area. On the way to growing up, they make countless mistakes. If you can remain cool-headed, you can begin to set the right tone.

Carole, the physician from California, for instance, who refused to tell her son George about her breast cancer, learned from her mistake. A few years later, she found herself and her younger son Judson in a situation that was far less grave, but no less important to discuss. She gave it some thought, then decided to bring the subject up at the dinner table, which was usually the only time of day when her family was together.

"You know what happened to me today?" she said, as all eyes at the table turned in her direction. "I was driving along the freeway going about 60 miles per hour, when, out of nowhere, a car came zooming across two lanes, wound its way around every other car in its path, and then narrowly missed me as it took off. I was terrified."

Everyone seemed aghast, especially Judson, who was outraged that anyone would put his wonderful mother's life at risk. He stopped chewing and said, "That was terrible, Mom. I'm glad you're okay."

"You're right, Judson," she answered, "it was terrible. But it's even worse; I know who the driver was."

Now everyone had stopped chewing. "It was you, Judson," she said calmly. After a long pause, she added, "So I'm sure you can understand why I have to take your car from you for two weeks, and why you'll have to take the bus."

Another mother told me she sat in shock as her 14-year-old daughter tried on the new skirt she'd bought. It was a denim mini, and this woman said the hemline reached a good seven inches above her daughter's knees. "There was a pleat in the back that jumped up when she walked," the woman said later. "I wanted to insist she take it off, but I didn't. I just sat there watching her."

Finally, her daughter turned to her, "You think it's too extreme, don't you?" she asked.

"You know I do, but—" her mother said, rubbing her hands together and searching for the right words, trying to decide if she should keep her opinions to herself or speak out. Then she began again, "I saw you in a new light last week when you were baby-sitting. You had all that trouble and no adults to turn to for help. You handled that so well, from alerting the police to leaving a note on the door for the baby's parents. You were cool-headed and mature. So I think that when it comes to something like this, whether or not you should wear that skirt, the decision should be yours."

At first the mother worried that she'd failed her daughter, that she should have given her a firmer response. She knew that teenagers, especially when their bodies begin to develop, typically test the boundaries of acceptable behavior on various levels. She thought this might be a particularly important time for her parental guidance and that she'd side-stepped the opportunity.

A week later, however, she knew she'd used the right approach when her daughter announced that she was returning the skirt. The mother asked what had prompted the decision and the girl said, "I may not have the personality for a skirt like this. The pleat in the back shows everything."

In both cases, the situation with the skirt, as well as the reckless driving, the mothers had three important aspects in common in their approach:

1) They gave themselves time before they spoke.
2) They began their narratives with feedback on how they felt. You'll find that keeping the emphasis on yourself, rather than trying to interpret your youngster's feelings, can help you diffuse a potentially explosive situation. Remember, the best way to approach a narrative is to visualize yourself pointing a finger, not at your child, but at yourself.
3) Rather than trying for retaliatory strikes, the parents framed their answers within the context of their long-range goals for their youngsters. The girl was encouraged to be mature. The young driver was shown his mistake from someone else's point of view. He was able to see that driving recklessly would not only endanger his life, but the lives of innocent people also.

It's not just these two parents. I'm often impressed with the creative approaches parents have come up with so they can communicate more effectively with their kids. Let me share some of their methods with you. You may discover one that works just right for your family.

One woman in Atlanta, who is a single parent, says that some sensitive subjects embarrass her two teenage boys so much that they are unable to fully participate in conversations with her. She has, therefore, begun introducing "taboo" subjects in a room with the lights turned out. That way, her boys know she can't see their faces. It seems to work, whether they're in the living room, with a blaze going in the fireplace, or at bedtime, just before her sons go to sleep. They talk "about almost any old thing," she says.

Another mother, this one in New Mexico, returned home from work and found her house unusually quiet. She called out for her 15-year-old daughter, but there was no response. Something told this woman there was something amiss in her house. She headed for her daughter's bedroom. There the girl sat, at her desk, a textbook open. Although she and her daughter had a casual conversation, every bone in this mother's body told her something was wrong. She turned to leave but stopped at the girl's closet and yanked the door open. There stood a boy from the neighborhood, his clothes in disarray.

"I was furious," the mother said. Heat shot to her head as if she'd been plugged into an electrical outlet, and it charged her emotions. But did she shout? Curse at the boy? Call her daughter names?

"I left the room as quickly as I could," the woman said. "I went to the living room, fell on my knees, and asked God for guidance. I knew that whatever I said to my daughter would be so important and would make such a lasting impression, for good or bad, and I wanted my words to come from a different place, not from my anger."

Writing It Out

Another woman, an anchorwoman from northern California, is the mother of two teenage girls. In the past year, the family has undergone emotional turmoil due to this woman's 19-year marriage ending in divorce. So much was happening so quickly in her home that she asked her daughters to write a letter to her about what they were feeling.

The oldest daughter turned out to be an extremely competent writer and, over the years, has written dozens of letters to her mother. In one, the girl discussed her uneasiness about going away to college.

She was frightened, she said, because "I don't know where I begin and you leave off."

Another approach that involves writing, may be more suitable for kids who aren't Shakespeares at heart. It was tried by another parent from northern California who works as a labor mediator.

This man, Barry, was having trouble getting his 17-year-old son, Seth, to come home on time. The first few times Seth was late, his father panicked, thought the worst. Then he began to believe Seth was taking advantage of his relaxed parenting style, and Barry decided to set some limits.

The next time the boy came home late Barry was waiting for him. "I said, 'Enough, you can't go out next weekend. You're grounded.'"

His son, who Barry now realized, in the heat of his anger, had grown as tall as he, walked up close to him. They stood menacingly nose to nose. Seth said to his father, "I'll get even with you for this."

Barry snarled back, "I don't feed my enemies." He threatened to throw his son out of the house if he didn't obey. Before the evening was over, though, Barry was feeling uncomfortable with the way he'd handled the matter. "I don't want to win an argument with him," Barry said. "I want to do what's right for him."

At that point, he sat down and devised a strategy to get his son talking, even when they are still angry with one another. He says it is based upon a standard mediation technique and he agreed to share it with us for this book. It works as follows.

Let your youngster choose a room or a time when you can sit down together to work out a solution to your differences. By allowing your teenager to choose the location, you're conveying the message that you're not imposing your will over him. He might well choose his bedroom, the one place that he considers his own personal space, or a favorite spot in your home. Just make sure it's someplace where there is a table or desk that you can both write on.

Have, at hand, pens or pencils and paper, with a sheet of carbon paper in the middle, for both of you. You will both now answer the following questions.

1. What do you like best about the other person? (Be prepared for your child to balk at this. When someone is angry he's obviously not inclined to say something nice about you. But this is an important piece of the strategy. Forcing yourself to think of something you admire in that other person reduces the level of hostility.)

2. Name one thing you dislike about this person. (Your child will begin scribbling madly here.)
3. What would you like to see this person do differently?
4. What, specifically, do you think the other person wants you to change? That is, what is it you're doing now that's making the other person angry?
5. Why do you do what you do? What's in it for you to continue?
6. Why do you think the other person wants you to change?
7. What do you think the other person wants you to do to make this work?
8. Is that possible? Why?
9. What do you think the other person has to do in order to make it work?
10. What are you willing to do to make peace?

At this point, after you've both finished writing, exchange papers so that each of you is left with your original copy and a copy of the other person's sheet. Take turns reading your answers aloud.

This approach helps to shed the light of reason on your argument. For example, Seth was forced to take a closer look at the situation. Basically, he wrote that he knows his father tries to be fair with him. He said he's embarrassed when his father begins calling and searching for him when he's late. Despite that, he continued, he liked staying out late because it made him feel like a man, someone more in control of his life. He said he knew his parents wanted him to come home because they worry that something terrible might happen to him. In the end, he said the best way to resolve the conflict would be to come home on time, but he asked, in turn, for his parents to begin treating him more like an adult.

According to Barry, this mediation approach enabled him and his son to enter into a healthy discussion of their conflicts. Both of them usually had to compromise some, but the problem was resolved and the negative behavior was turned around.

As you can see, mediation is quite democratic, as is the next approach. In fact, it seems to have been lifted straight from the pages of a Democratic caucusing book. It involves breaking up into small family groups before a general family meeting is held.

Household Democracy

This method is suggested by a psychologist in Montana whom I will call Chip. His family members had been through a divorce, relocation, and remarriage. When Chip, his new wife, and his children got together, he found that while there was a lot of talking occurring, there was a dearth of real communication.

"It's important to remember that a disruption in your house, can affect you deeply, sometimes to the core of the child still within you. To understand your feelings at such a time, you may need to examine your emotional development."

Chip used himself as an example. He said his mother had been raised by a cruel stepmother and when she became a parent herself, she was frightened of harshness or anger and had a laissez-faire approach to child-rearing. Chip said he followed his mother's example. "I avoided confrontation with my children. I wanted to be their friend, and that meant when they were with me there was little structure."

That became a real problem for his new wife, Carolyn, who was snubbed by Chip's children. The son, Mark, would not speak to her for long stretches of time, and when he did speak, he made snide comments or acted unruly at the dinner table.

Chip tried ignoring the young man's behavior, but not surprisingly, this upset Carolyn all the more. How was Chip to remain true to his own nonconfrontational nature, while, at the same time, helping bring about peace in his family?

First, they tried holding family meetings. "That didn't work at all," Chip said, "because they put everyone on the defensive. What we needed was a way to deal with what was going on below the surface."

He thought the family meetings might work better if everyone broke up into smaller groups to stimulate conversation. "We just did it again recently," said Chip. "It was during the holidays, so we were all home together and Carolyn became tense and irritable. Her mood cast a chill over everyone else's holiday."

His daughter, now skilled at the family technique, came to Chip. "We need to talk," she said to him. "I really hate it when Carolyn acts like this. She has always done it and it makes me feel lonely and not welcome in this house."

Her father encouraged her to share her feelings with Carolyn, who was disturbed by her stepdaughter's reaction, but agreed to keep the conversation going. She then turned to the son, Mark, for feedback. Mark told her he understood her irritation. He said he'd been depressed during the holidays, but felt he couldn't let his sister know, and had only been smiling for her sake. Round and round their talk went, each family member shared their feelings and thoughts with one another.

Then they were ready for a group meeting. Carolyn opened the conversation by sharing some of her memories about what holidays had been like in her home, when she was a kid, and how this might have affected her mood. She also expressed some of her anger about situations that had occurred between her and the family recently. Then, the daughter talked of her bitterness over past holidays, after her father had left her mother. She said that after the divorce she'd felt abandoned by him, that holidays had been terrible times for her because her mother, trying to cope with the separation, had been an emotional wreck. Everyone talked and shared feelings about their recent holidays. The conversation lasted more than an hour. No one was offering advice and telling the others what to do. Instead, everyone was expected to contribute the gift of truth.

"We were talking about what was really going on in our home," Chip said. And when it was over, there was much that was unanswered and even some residual anger and resentment. But later Chip said, "I saw my daughter standing at a counter and I went over and gave her a big hug. She hugged me back. I had to resist trying to make everything wonderful for her. I knew I couldn't. Some problems can't be solved. But at least by talking we were able to move on to general expressions of affection. We were trusting enough to let what we felt come to the surface. That meant anger as well as love. I trust in this. I know our love for one another is real and genuine."

Why did it work? Well, if you'll notice, they talked about genuine feelings and their individual responses to a situation. They did not hurl accusations at one another.

This method, like anything new, requires practice and patience before getting it right. When everyone is annoyed and uptight, it's difficult not to lash out. But if you and your teenager can learn to keep the focus on yourselves, each of you talking about how you feel in an open and honest exchange, you'll almost hear the walls in your house come tumbling down.

I've given you many ideas about how to begin anew with your teenager. Next, let's consider how you can begin to commit to these changes.

What Teens Say:
"Parents Drive Us Crazy When They . . ."

(Each phrase or sentence represents a new voice.)

- "Complain about how hard it is to be a parent."
- "Leave their things lying around the house."
- "Say nothing when you know they know you did wrong."
- "They are penny pinchers."
- "Talk about their jobs at dinner."
- "Won't give you a reason why they said no before hearing you out."
- "Bully you."
- "Are happy when telling me I can't do something."
- "Talk about your problems with other adults."
- "Mispronounce names."
- "Throw subtle and sarcastic jabs at you."
- "Never give you a one-word answer."
- "Talk to my friends on the phone."
- "Act like teenagers."
- "Put words in your mouth."
- "Won't let you leave the table until you've eaten things you hate."
- "Smoke (I thought it was adults who were supposed to be the smart ones)."
- "Would rather buy me things than talk to me."
- "Give me a guilt trip when I do something wrong."
- "Treat you like you're much younger than you are."
- "Fire questions until I'm totally annoyed."
- "Come home from work and don't want to talk, just read the paper and watch TV."
- "Lecture me. I've never been punished, but mental punishment is harder to take than physical punishment."
- "Tell me to straighten up my room."
- "Embarrass me when they're trying to be funny."
- "Tell their friends about all the trouble you get into."
- "Tell me how good I have it and how bad they had it."
- "Talk to themselves out loud."
- "Try to live their lives through you."

- "Put down teenagers."
- "Think teenagers' lives are all fun and games."
- "Expect you to be just like them."
- "Ignore the brilliant and (always better) incredibly fantastic ideas of students."
- "Make generalizations that youth are irresponsible, stupid, etc."
- "Tell you to shut up."
- "Say, 'I never did that when I was your age.'"
- "Preach values which don't apply to the present."
- "Nag about homework—even though I already have a 4.0 average."
- "Go in my room and mess things up."
- "Spit at each other."
- "Give me false hopes, empty promises, and straight out lies."
- "Get involved when I am fighting with my brother, and don't even know what they're talking about."
- "Tend to be hypocritical in their use of alcohol."
- "Try to act cool when my friends are around."
- "Pick their noses while driving."
- "Call when I am in the middle of something and keep bugging me until I stop what I'm doing so I can help."
- "Wear ugly clothing."
- "Get drunk."
- "Treat me like a baby."
- "Don't trust me."
- "Nag."
- "Act like parents."
- "Constantly have to know where I am."
- "Say, 'Do you want a punch in the nose?'"
- "Ignore me."
- "Argue over which courses I'll take."
- "Joke with their friends about how happy they'll be when I go away to college."
- "Act like all teenagers are thieves, drug addicts, and alcoholics."
- "Put me in the middle of their fights."
- "Don't explain what they mean."
- "Discount my opinions."
- "Ask, 'Did you do this?' and although you say no, they keep asking until they get the answer they want."

- "Watch TV every night and fall asleep—no time to talk."
- "Try to be your best friend."
- "Think they're always right."
- "Fuss with my personal stuff."
- "Repeat themselves a lot."
- "Make life hell for me if I make a mistake."
- "Fight with each other and take it out on my sister and me."
- "Act like a workaholic."
- "Try to live my life for me."
- "Ask me to tell them about my boyfriends."
- "Get angry with me and I feel dead inside."
- "Put down today's fads, fashions, and music."
- "Expect to know about every aspect of your life."
- "Say that I'm stupid."
- "Try to force me to talk."
- "Call me shorty."
- "Tell me to act like an adult and treat me like a child."
- "Say they can do stuff but I can't—it's hypocritical."
- "Compare me to other people."
- "Never talk to me and I wish I knew them better, but now I'm afraid to know."
- "Take away privileges like the car if I don't get straight As."
- "Refuse to lose weight."
- "Try to figure out what's wrong when they don't know anything."
- "Embarrass me."
- "Tell me how to live my life even though theirs is screwed up."
- "Insist they told me things they didn't."

6

Commitment Is
The Key

By now you realize that to make your relationship work with your teenager, you must say "no" to your old story of mistrust, and "yes" to starting and maintaining a new approach to communication. This will require far more, however, than your good intentions.

What Commitment Really Means

Let's say you walk into your teenager's room, see her lying on the floor unconscious, and nearby there's an empty bottle, marked "poison." You rush to the phone, dial emergency, but the number just rings and rings. Then what do you do? You rush to a neighbor's house, bang on the door, but no answer. You try more doors. Still no answers. You try the phone again, this time dialing zero. But the operator gives you a hard time. It's not fair, you think. But there's no time to complain. Every moment counts.

This actually happened to a woman who found her child on the brink of death. She had nothing on but her nightie and it was freezing outside. After trying the phone, she ran outside anyway. When she couldn't reach a neighbor or get help on the phone, she ran into the middle of a busy street. Cars screeched to a stop, and she told people what was happening. They took her and her child to the hospital. She saved her child's life.

Now that is commitment. She took every single and solitary step necessary to save her child's life. Remind yourself that this book is your opportunity to save your child's future. Find the courage to commit to change.

Practice, Don't Preach

Be prepared not to get it right the first time. One woman I worked with, whom I shall call Marie, felt she had done a thorough job evaluating her core issues and was ready to rewrite her family's story. Then, out of the blue, a conflict emerged between her and her 16-year-old son, David. When it had ended, "I was so disappointed with myself," Marie said. "I used all the same old words again. Everything was wrong."

Despite your best intentions, your temper or your old habits may get in the way of your plans. Don't give up. You haven't failed. You've taken the first step in a journey of a thousand. Mastery will only come after repetition. If you don't try though, you'll never learn.

I suggested to Marie that since she had identified her core issues and had taken a clear look at them, she already knew which subjects were especially difficult for her to discuss with her son. I made the following suggestions to her.

1. Start again by explaining to David how these issues evolved in your life. Explain through a personal narrative that can conclude with, "so that's why I act that way when you and I get into a conflict about. . . ." (Share your dreams, aspirations, fears, concerns, and what you see as important issues between people, especially you and your teen.)
2. Announce your plan concerning what you can do so your core issues cannot continue to fuel heightened tension between you and your son.

She did this, then went a step further. "I wrote my core issues down on big pieces of cardboard, with the words 'homework' and 'classroom behavior' spelled out." They hung the signs, which they called "code blues," in several rooms as visual reminders. The problem came up again. But even with the signs posted, they forgot all about them—at first.

"I was half-way into one of my lectures about how he'd let me down, when David pointed to the sign," Marie said. It had been drawn with crayon on brown cardboard and it didn't make for easy reading.

Still, they both knew exactly what the words meant. "My son had been covering his ears, saying 'please stop yelling.' I hadn't stopped. I was so caught up in my own self-righteousness. He was wrong. I was right. He deserved to be scolded, I was thinking."

When her son pointed to the sign they both stopped speaking. "It was as if my whole life flashed before my eyes," she said. "I saw myself in junior high, working so hard to get the best grades. I wanted everyone to think I was perfect. And everyone else might have thought so, but I sure didn't. Now here I was with my son, wanting his teachers to see me as the perfect mother, with a son who made excellent grades. I guess I felt, how dare you spoil the image."

She made an appointment with her son so they could deal with the school problem when they both had more control over themselves. "At least I got it halfway right that time," she concluded.

Parents often ask me whether they should simply initiate a new approach with their youngsters, without mentioning why. I always say no. Don't leave your teenagers in the dark. That's the coward's way out. There's only one way to begin communicating effectively . . . with the right words and a desire to improve the relationship. Remember, the "how you do it" is as important as what you do—your tone of voice, your willingness to listen and acknowledge your teen's point of view, and then tell how it is for you.

Don't Wait Until It's Too Late

One woman in Connecticut almost waited until it was too late. Jenny was concerned about her teenage son Todd's rebellious behavior. "It got to a point where if I had asked him to keep breathing he would have stood there and held his breath until he turned blue," she said.

She worried that he'd become too reckless, especially when it came to a bridge in their quiet town. This bridge was a popular hang-out for local kids. When the weather grew warm, some of the more daring boys dived from it into the river below. The first time she heard her son talking about it she warned him of the possible dangers. "He swore to me he'd never do anything like that," she said.

Her worst fears were realized, however, when she received a call from the police. Her son had dived off the bridge and been badly injured. When she arrived at the hospital she learned that he'd broken his neck as well as his legs and arms.

"It was such a stupid thing for him to have done," she said, but she only said that to herself. "I figured he had to realize how foolish he'd been. It certainly wasn't going to do either of us any good if I told him that when he was lying in a hospital bed."

The young man spent months recuperating. "I visited him every day," she said. "Much of the time we were just too drained to speak." When he finally began healing, they started talking again but not in the same old way. His near-tragedy forced them to change their story. "His father was working and my other kids were in school, so it was usually just the two of us," she said. "I suppose that forced us to see one another differently. When we began talking again we connected."

Starting Over Again

No one wants to wait for a calamity to arise before they start communicating. The time to start is now. Consider what you want to tell your youngster about starting over again. You'll want to combine your personal narrative with the following points:

1. Admit the old way of trying to communicate was a failure.
2. Ask your youngster if he agrees, and find out . . . "What was it like for you?" "What made it hard, easy, good or bad for you?"
3. Acknowledge and affirm his perception: "I can see where that would hurt." "That must have been really frustrating." "I never knew that's how it was for you!"
4. Pause— be silent for a moment—avoid rushing to find a remedy or make things better immediately.
5. Offer some examples of times when you've known something was working in your life and times when you've had to admit failure.
6. Explain how your past may have impacted your relationship.
7. Share your hopes. What would be ideal for you in establishing successful communication?

Recalling Your Past

Once again, if you're having difficulty selecting a personal narrative and have trouble recalling incidents from your life, try starting a journal. Begin with your earliest memory. Where were you? Who might have been with you? If you work your way through most of the years of your life, up to and including the present, you'll find that your memory bank is slowly opening.

If that fails, try categorizing. Make a list of relatives, different houses you lived in. Look through family albums. Write down the names of towns you lived in, schools you attended. Another list should include memorable holidays, vacations, as well as family tragedies and battles.

Should you still find yourself unable to recall events from your past, play reporter. Interview yourself. Write down questions in a notebook and follow them up with answers. Don't know what questions to ask? Start with the simple who, what, when, where, and how. Who, for instance, were your parents? This might be answered by including where they came from, what their parents were like, etc. When you've answered all the "who" questions, move on to what. This might apply to your immediate past. What was your childhood like? Did you live in poverty? Did both your parents work at jobs outside the home?

If you try jogging your memory in this manner for a few minutes at a time, you'll find that you have hundreds of questions and hundreds of answers. If, for instance, you say your mother worked outside the home try to remember how she felt about that and how it impacted your life.

It's never too late to start again. Clara, a woman from Brooklyn, New York said her conversations with her 18-ycar-old daughter Denise had deteriorated to monosyllables. She found empty beer bottles scattered on the floor beneath the young woman's bed, and the mother was always angry about the loud rock music her daughter played.

Then there was the issue of the girl's looks. She refused to dress in anything but black. She dyed her hair blue black, and shaved a patch out of the back of her head, as well as a piece of her eyebrows. "I hated even having to look at her," her mother said.

The feeling seemed to be mutual. "Denise announced that she wanted to move out and get an apartment with some friends," the woman said. She didn't resist her daughter's plans; in fact, she was delighted. But the week before she was scheduled to go, her mother realized that she didn't want them to part with their relationship in such a sorry state.

After thinking carefully about what she wanted to say to her daughter, she suggested that before the girl moved they could go bowling together. They did, and when they came out of the bowling alley, the mother took advantage of one of their rare light-hearted moments together to talk.

"I told her it made me nervous to talk about my feelings," Clara said. "I started forgetting everything I planned to say. I just blurted things out, but I think she got the message."

As they walked together down city streets, Clara began by pointing to a car that drove by. In essence, she said she wished she had the same power a traffic light has. "I'd just say stop," she told Denise. "Stop hurting each other, stop being disrespectful to each other." She added that she didn't have the power to stop by herself, but that they could together. "The only way I know how to get along with a kid is the way I learned when I was a kid myself. It didn't work for your grandparents and it isn't working for me."

Denise had been walking with her, not saying a word. Clara wondered if she was making any sense at all. Denise stopped walking and made eye contact. Clara told her they could find a new way to talk to one another, that they could leave the old way right there on the street and walk away from it. The girl didn't answer, not with words anyway. "Her eyes just filled with tears and she put her arms around me," Clara said.

"There we were in the middle of Manhattan. She was crying. I wouldn't have believed it. I cried also. When we stopped I had black gook all over my jacket from her make-up." At the corner, they paused for a traffic light. Clara thought that was rather symbolic in terms of what she expected for them in the future. They would have a lot of stops and starts. They couldn't change overnight. But they'd move toward a new relationship together.

Now is the perfect time for you to stop and consider how you can move into the future with your teenager. And don't just think about it. Telling your youngster of your hopes and dreams means you're already moving in the right direction.

There are many parents who had success with their teenagers and can serve as inspiration for all of us. So, in our next chapter, we'll take a look at what successful parents do, so we can learn from them.

HIGH PRAISE
What Teens Say:
"My Greatest Compliment for My Parents Is . . ."

(Each sentence represents a new voice.)

- "They love each other a lot and get along well, which makes living with them easier."
- "They listen to me."
- "I don't have a compliment for them."
- "They're the greatest."
- "I can talk with them about my problems."
- "They help me excel to my fullest."
- "They get along well with other people."
- "They support most of my ideas."
- "They hardly ever yell."
- "They have raised me well."
- "They are understanding (sometimes)."
- "They care and show it."
- "My mom stayed home with me until I was in the sixth grade."
- "They pretty much allow me to make my own decisions."
- "They give me a room to sleep in and food to eat."
- "They're always available."
- "I know she loves me."
- "They make me work for what I want so I will appreciate it."
- "My mom is the best, my dad is a nothing."
- "My mom loves me no matter what I do, and that's cool."
- "They have good jobs."
- "My mom is very intelligent."
- "They are not too strict."
- "They are my best friends and we talk about everything."
- "She understands me."
- "They're awesome."
- "They give me good meals."
- "They trust me."
- "My mom is good looking."
- "They do the best they can."
- "They are my heroes."

- "I am here."
- "They say they love me."
- "They're very involved."
- "They're nice to my friends."
- "They're lovable."
- "I like them a lot."
- "You're doing a great job, Mom and Dad—keep it up!"
- "We solve problems together."
- "They continue to support me, regardless."
- "They tell me I am very special to them."
- "They tell me all the time that they love me."
- "They respect my opinions."
- "My dad is the best because he understands."
- "They're patient."
- "They are my role models."
- "They love me soooooooo much."
- "They give me privacy."
- "My mother is beautiful."
- "I love them."
- "They are always there when I need them."
- "Thank you for keeping me in line."
- "They would sacrifice everything for my siblings and me."
- "My dad's honest and my mom's fun."
- "They believe in me."
- "They think I have really high potential."
- "They provide for me."
- "No words are good enough to compliment my parents."
- "They are the most understanding and supportive people in my life."
- "I could not ask for better parents."
- "They had me."
- "They know how to survive."
- "My mother has raised me by herself and has done a great job."
- "They are motivators."
- "They're easy to talk to."
- "My father believes in me."
- "My mom is trustworthy and my dad is supportive."
- "Mom and Dad, you are the best thing that ever happened to me."
- "They are the most unselfish people in the world."
- "Thank you for devoting so much time to me."

- "My mother has good manners."
- "They have taught me to believe in myself."
- "They love me for who I am."
- "They give me room to grow."
- "Thank you, Mom and Dad, for getting through the first 18 years of my life."
- "If I ever marry, I want to have a marriage like theirs."

Habits of
Successful Parents

Judging from what you've read so far, you'd think I believe teenagers are nothing but trouble. That couldn't be farther from the truth. Each day I am heartened by the hundreds of bright and promising young people I meet who are sure to lead America into one of its most progressive centuries. In fact, I've been looking forward to introducing you to one young person in particular.

One Youngster's Success Story

Nichele Guiton, of Falls Church, Virginia, represents so many of the bright and eager young people I've met, but whose stories I haven't room to include here. Nichele reflects not only many of their qualities, but those we all hope to see in our own youngsters. She is honorable, personable, optimistic, and self-confident. She is also a great academic success at the University of Virginia, where she is majoring in English.

Her folks were not only good parents, but successful ones. And I'm making that distinction for a reason. I'm sure you're a good parent. That's why you're taking time to read this book and follow through on some of the suggestions. You want the best for your youngster. But you can't take credit for that. Wanting the best for them comes naturally. Success in raising them does not; that involves behavior modification and well thought out strategies tailored to you and your youngster's individual needs. Nichele's mother, Bonnie Guiton, who has recently been appointed to California Governor Pete Wilson's cabinet, has certainly done something right in the parenting department, just as Nichele's dad, Harvie, has. Unfortunately I could not discuss his daughter with him. He died two years ago. But it turns out that the best person to consult, as to what the Guitons did right, is Nichele herself. At 21, she is still close enough to adolescence to remember most of the details of her upbringing, yet far enough away from it to offer us a mature assessment of why her teenage years with her parents were almost free from strife.

Here's what Nichele had to say: "My parents worked hard at giving me a sense of control over my own life. I was encouraged to make a lot of decisions myself." Nichele said when it came to something like clothing, her mother didn't dictate. "When I walked out wearing something she didn't approve of, she'd ask whether I felt comfortable in it. She wasn't telling me to take it off, but suggesting that I give it more thought. She'd let me make the decision."

Nichele said her parents were not afraid to use the "no" word. "But they usually saved it for issues that were life threatening," she added.

What's more, she believes her parents' democratic style—which stressed that every opinion counted in their household, including Nichele's—will make a difference in how she handles herself in the workplace. She graduated recently and hopes to work her way up into a leadership position in the public relations field.

She firmly believes she can help make this a better world to live in. At the time of the interview, she had her career plans mapped out like an explorer charting new and unopened territories. And she didn't seem in the least intimidated by her array of choices. "It's all so exciting," she said, "and it's up to me to make the right decisions."

Later in this chapter, I'll give you more on that democratic parenting style that Nichele's folks employed, and explain why and how it works. For now though, it's important to note that, when given the opportunity to name several strategies that her parents employed, Nichele emphasized their ability to relinquish control over minor everyday issues, like her choice of clothing.

Twelve Vital Habits

I agree with her. In fact, the subject of parental control and the need to let go is so important that I've devoted the next chapter to it. So, for the time being, let's simply make "letting go" the first item on our list of habits of successful parents. All together, this list will include 12 strategies for you to consider and practice until they become habitual. First, I'll give you a quick rundown of the other eleven, then follow up with explanations. So, in addition to

1. Relinquish control of minor issues, a successful parents learns to:
2. Look beyond the "headline" news in a teenager's life.

"Headline" news is any teenage action or comment designed to get your attention. It makes you take notice. Often, teenagers use this tactic with their clothing, hairstyles, friends, language, or music. You may consider their choices to be in bad taste, disconcerting, or irrational.

A successful parent doesn't overreact to this. Your best defense is to stop, think, and take time to figure out the real story behind the headline. (Part of the story has to do with the fact that most teenagers at some point test the limit of, or rebel against, normal standards of protocol, decorum and the values of their parents.)

One woman, named Sheila, said she recently received a phone call from her 13-year-old son's guidance counselor. The boy, Paul, had been thrown out of class by his English teacher because he was interrupting the teacher's lecture with sarcastic remarks.

Rather than respond to the counselor, Sheila asked him to put her son on the phone. She'd heard the headline news and was searching for the small print of the story. Rather than a rebuke, her first words to her son were, "How are you feeling right now?"

She also asked Paul for his version of the story. When he'd corroborated the charges against him, Sheila calmly told Paul she disapproved of his behavior and that they would discuss it when he returned from school. Then, before talking to the counselor again, she communicated an important message to her son, which told him that her feelings were unconditional. She simply said to the boy, "I love you."

Later that same afternoon, when Sheila went to get the mail, she found a card that Paul had clandestinely sent to his father, who lived in another state. It was returned by the mail carrier and stamped "moved, no forwarding address."

Sheila began to recall that, in recent weeks, Paul had been running to the mailbox, checking to see if there was a letter for him. When she asked if he was expecting to hear from anyone, he always replied that no, he was not. But she could tell from the desperate words on this returned card that he had obviously been trying to reach his dad, who, over the years, had proved unreliable.

She realized her son's acting out in class probably had something to do with his frustration over his father. "It didn't mean I excused Paul's behavior, but it helped me understand it," Sheila said. She was glad that she'd not overreacted.

3. Listen (even when it means biting your lip) so your youngster can tell his side of the story and feel heard before you respond.

We must examine what it means to be a good listener. We all know this isn't as easy as it sounds. In fact, it involves two steps. First, you must offer your youngster the gift of silence while she tries to make her point. When you're annoyed, it's easy to just bowl your youngster over with what you've got to say, then refuse to listen.

A lot of parents scold or yell, and when their teenagers respond with words and actions that are equally as angry, rude, or sarcastic, the parents accuse them of impertinence.

Learning to be silent and listen can be as difficult as walking across hot coals. It hurts. But both are disciplines that can be learned. I meant it when I said that you might have to start out by biting your lip. Any physical restraint could do the trick. Try holding your breath, if necessary, or placing a crooked index finger on your mouth.

The second step in the art of listening is to interpret aloud that which you believe your youngster has said. You might begin with the words, "Let me make sure I understand you correctly. You think. . . ."

Then you listen again while your youngster tells you whether you've got it right. One technique I often use is the "single word question" such as . . . "Hurt?" . . . "Angry?" . . . "Frustrated?" Then, pause. These help open a door to more discussion. This is especially true when followed up with an acknowledgment of their response to the question, such as . . . "I can understand why you do what you do . . ." or "It does not make it easy, does it?"

Use these questions only as prompts to get more information and to find a common ground for sharing. These approaches do not mean that you agree or disagree for that is not the purpose here. You are only looking for common ground on which to develop and maintain rapport. These are signals that you are listening and trying to understand.

4. Incorporate personal narratives into casual conversations, do not reserve them strictly for troubled times.

You may never be able to deliver your story with an impassioned oratorical style. But as I said earlier, that's not important. Learning to share stories, rather than scolding, lecturing, or shaming, is vital. And it's just as essential that you learn to weave those tales into pleasant conversations. You don't want your child to associate your storytelling with troubled times. It's supposed to be a pleasurable experience for you both. How do you get started? Let me give you an example.

One man, whom we shall call Bill, had become so adept at the personal narratives approach, that he began to craft his stories spontaneously. A while back, in fact, Bill invited his sixteen-year-old son, whom we shall call Jason, to see the movie "Scenes From A Mall," starring Bette Midler and Woody Allen. When the movie ended, Jason looked at his dad, rolled his eyes, and said, "That was boring."

Bill was silent for a moment, then he asked Jason why he hadn't liked the movie. "Well, it wasn't funny," Jason said. His father nodded his head in agreement, and before he realized it, he began to weave a story:

BILL: The review in this morning's paper said it wasn't funny but I wanted to see it anyway. I admire Woody Allen's integrity.

JASON: How do you know about his integrity?

BILL: I read that 30 years ago, he gave up a writing job that paid $1,700 a week, for a $50 a week gig, at a comedy club.

JASON: (Grinning) That integrity cost him a lot of money.

BILL: (Playfully punches his son in the arm) He obviously couldn't have afforded it if he'd had to feed you and Ryan (Jason's younger brother). In this story, it said that for a year and a half, Woody Allen was so awful, he'd deliver his jokes and not one person in the club would laugh. Can you imagine?

JASON: (Giggling) I can just see his diary. (He lowers his voice in jest.) Christmas comes, no one laughed tonight. Spring. There's still dead silence out there . . . And Dad, those were the nights when his relatives came. That's a righteous slap, pure embarrassment, crippling.

BILL: It's true. He knew what he wanted and kept plugging away no matter how it hurt.

JASON: It paid off, for sure. He's famous.

BILL: And people like me trust him. He always gives me something to think about.

JASON: That's like Sinead O'Connor. I don't always like what she sings, but I know it's important. You mean stuff like that, right?

BILL: Um hmm. I even got something from that movie tonight.

JASON: What?

BILL: Remember that scene when they were in the theater and Bette Midler started analyzing him right there?

JASON: Yeah.

BILL: She said he was trying to ruin their marriage because his own mother hadn't been good to him, so he didn't trust being in relationships with women. That's why he was destroying his marriage.

JASON: Yeah, so?

BILL: It made me think about when I've done that, with a friend I had and a teacher, once. You think you might do that sometimes?

JASON: No.

BILL: How about with Noel (his new wife, the boy's stepmother)?

JASON: I don't know. Yeah, sometimes.

BILL: Maybe because your mother died when you were so young. Maybe you're afraid Noel might leave us, too.

JASON: It was just a movie, Dad.

BILL: Does art imitate life or is it the other way around? What do you think?

JASON: I'm feeling kinda put on the spot. Can we talk about it another time?

BILL: I'd like that.

JASON: I'm hungry . . . Pizza?

BILL: (Nodding his head yes and smiling) Okay, pizza.

It was not a life changing story, but it was powerful enough to give young Jason something to think about. Bill conveyed two important messages to his son. The first was that, in the end, it's hard work, diligence, and a strong notion of self that helps us achieve our goals. Secondly, he opened the door to an important dialogue. Apparently, the boy and his stepmother had been experiencing some problems.

Rather than jump in the middle of the friction, when he saw it occurring at home, Bill waited until a lighter moment, then introduced the subject.

It was unplanned, but he was able to communicate his concern about the tension. He said his son may have, unwittingly, been trying to sabotage his relationship with Noel, the boy's stepmother. I'd say Bill got a lot of mileage out of those two movie tickets.

Best of all, toward the end of the conversation, when young Jason said he felt "put on the spot," it signaled us that he trusted his father enough to share his feelings. He obviously believed Bill would "hear" him and not take offense. Also, Bill allowed the conversation to end, without feeding his ego and presenting some grand moralistic conclusion to the story. He simply let it end, as he should have.

If he had instead "preached" the same messages to Jason, he could have probably gotten it out in half the time. The narrative certainly took longer, but I'm willing to bet, as I'm sure you are, that the chances for getting Jason to hear him were increased ten-fold.

In this same vein, the successful parent also passes down family lore. According to the *Oxford English Dictionary*, there are many definitions for the word lore. These include ". . . a teaching or instruction, . . . used with reference to moral principles, . . . advice . . . counsel . . . story."

The idea of passing down a family story which teaches moral principles, appears to be more popular in some cultures than in others. I had a conversation with K.C., a youngster of Japanese heritage, whose lineage could be traced back to the 16th century. K.C.'s head was full of stories about his ancestors. The one I remember best was about K.C.'s wealthy and privileged grandmother, who was forced, as a young woman living in China, to escape from her home with her children, in the dead of night, while a major military offensive raged around them. She walked for days carrrying her three children, and then one of her babies died.

Sadly, this woman dug a grave for her infant, and wrapped the sash of her silk kimono around him, praying it would keep him warm in his next life. She bid him goodbye and moved on. After five more days, during which she and her remaining children subsisted on worms and rats, a second child died, and again she dug a grave. Finally, days later, she was rescued by her countrymen, with her one remaining child strapped to her body. This woman, who had been served hand and foot by servants, amazed those who had known her. How, someone asked her, had she found the resolve to keep moving, despite her grief, hunger, and weariness?

"This child," she responded, holding her wailing infant high above her, "he is our future and he has been entrusted to my care. The idea of letting go of the future was unthinkable."

What a rich legacy for future generations. This family lore, which had been passed down to K.C. from his mother, told him something about who he was: an inheritor of the future. It said that K.C.'s days ought never be squandered, for he was filled with the blood of this courageous woman.

Of course not all of us have such dramatic tales to share with our children, to instruct, guide, and counsel them. Nor is it our custom, in America, to use our family stories. But let's try.

Aren't there some Depression stories in your ancestral trunk that you can dig up and shake off? Maybe your father sold apples on a street corner. Isn't it amazing that he had the strength to continue in the face of such adversity? What does that say about the character of your family? I see it as something to be proud of.

What else can you garner from this period of great impoverishment? Did your parents witness kindnesses, acts of heroism, some noble plans that worked? What about the way people looked and dressed in those days and how they spent their time?

They are all facts that can give your story some color. Give it some thought and as you do you will find yourself shaping it into a narrative worth sharing.

Remembering as You Create Lore

Now consider your lifetime. What incidents were you able to witness as your mother, father, or any relative did something humorous or with savvy?

Don't ignore the minor stories. Don't all of us have some aunt, mother, or sister who started her marriage as a terrible cook, and perhaps prepared a meal that was inedible? The blackened pot roast, the rubber chicken, the distressed bride—each of us has at least one of those stories in our history. What has happened? Can this same woman cook up a storm now? Doesn't this show some measure of determination? Or maybe she never learned to cook. Isn't it great that she tries anyway?

Your family lore is there but it may be disguised or buried. Keep looking for it, be open to it. Once you find the story, consider why it could be a meaningful offering to your youngster, then pass it on as you would any legacy. Sharing the lore will leave your child with a distinct impression of a wholesome, humorous, giving, or enduring family member who shared the values which matter to you today. As you tell your stories, they may only be fragments. But as your child looks back, she will probably view them as part of a great pattern that says, "This is who we are."

Before we move on, I want to share the story of Marlene, then show you how it can be used to its maximum potential. She insisted that she had no family lore, but when encouraged, she turned to some elderly relatives and began asking questions about her family.

Eventually, she learned about her great Aunt Marjorie. It's a story that could easily have been lost, but fortunately it was not.

Apparently, in her later years, great Aunt Marjorie used to sit at the window of her tenement, in the Bedford Stuyvesant section of Brooklyn, and sprinkle bread crumbs on the windowsill to feed pigeons. She did this every day for years, never missing a day, no matter how little money she had.

One night, so the story goes, Aunt Marjorie died, and it wasn't until the next day that one of her young nieces, Amy, remembered that the birds would be arriving any moment. She wanted to feed them as a gesture of love for her great aunt. Amy spread the crumbs on the sill, and closed the window, as she'd seen Aunt Marjorie do so many times before.

You know what? The birds didn't come. Not that day, or ever again. It was as if they knew their friend had died.

What a marvelous tale for Marlene, this woman who had cared enough to unearth this lore. She could tell her children about their great Aunt Marjorie, who, though sorely strapped for cash, always remembered God's smaller creatures. She loved them and they seemed to know it. As for the birds' failure to return? It can't be explained, and that's the beauty of it.

I believe that years from now, when Marlene or any of her children mention just a few words from the story, it will be like a familial code. When something occurs that seems inexplicable, all Marlene need do is say "like Great Aunt Marjorie." Her children will understand, as if they share a secret family language.

5. Offer predictability and consistency through participation (not simply attendance and going through the motions), in a religious institution or nonsectarian community group, as well as through shared family rituals.

Rituals offer predictability and consistency. They are ceremonies or rites, and we generally associate them with marriages, other religious or devotional services, birthdays, births, deaths, holidays, etc. Although your family may participate in these events, they may leave you feeling unphased. For that reason, a lot of successful parents have created their own family rituals that meet their emotional needs.

What is most surprising about these families' rituals is that they are often not recognized as rituals at all. One family participates in several spring walk-a-thons each year. They all walk together, wearing tee shirts that are imprinted with their surname, and a logo, which is created by a young family member. They raise money for various causes from neighbors, colleagues, and classmates. Members of the family begin training together on weekends, during February and March.

Another family gets together twice a month and prepares a pot of chili. Another family collects the names and numbers of the sick and shut-ins from a nearby rest home, and, on New Year's Eve, when so many of these people would be forgotten, they phone them to wish God's blessings throughout the New Year.

No matter how complex or simple, rituals are important. Consider them the heartbeat of a family's life. Our youngsters have come to rely on the feelings of warmth they engender, and as they shape their own stories about who they are, these rituals will be fondly remembered.

Sydney Metrick, co-author of *The Art of Ritual*, published by Celestial Arts in Berkeley, California, said that since teenagers are so uncertain about their future, rituals are important "even if it's something they commonly reject, such as a religious tradition, they still need some form of a family ritual. They need to know that some things are going to remain the same."

Metrick and her co-author, Renee Beck, recommend that parents of adolescents create rituals that address the changes taking place in their youngsters. As an example, Metrick suggested that the teenager be given three boxes to decorate. "One can be filled with all the items the teenager no longer wants or identifies with. The second can be a transition box for things he's not involved with, but wants to keep, like a Little League cap. And the third box is marked 'in flux.' This is for the teenager to share with the family," Metrick continued. "It tells who he is at that time."

Family members can have occasional ceremonies, offering small gifts to put in that box. They can say to the teenager, "I honor and respect who you are."

Another woman, whose son became interested in environmental causes, contacted the local forestry service, and she and her son began selling live Christmas trees. "When the holidays were over the trees were replanted in our local park," she said. "We were able to raise enough extra money to buy several more for planting. It was the best Christmas we ever had together and we hope to do this every year. It's my way of telling him I share his concerns."

6. Admit fallibility. This includes apologizing for mistakes and admitting you don't always have quick solutions to dilemmas.

Think about a mistake you may have made recently. Perhaps you accused your teenager of some act that he was later found not to be guilty of. Or maybe he was, but you still hate the way you reacted. Let's face it, as parents, we're bound to make mistakes, and many of them.

All that we can do, when they occur, is apologize and move on. Sometimes though, simply saying "I'm sorry" isn't enough. That is especially the case when we've fallen back into an old behavior pattern.

The rule is this. An explosive accusation requires an equally powerful apology. I don't mean begging forgiveness. But for your sake, as well as your teen's, you should attempt to explain why you acted the way you did—and speak from your heart, not your head.

Don't say, for instance, "I screamed at you in front of your friends because you should have let me know where you would be."

Talk instead about how you felt, and where those feelings might have come from. For example, "I was so frightened when I couldn't find you. I kept imagining all sorts of things. I was wrong and I'm sorry."

7. Maintain a sense of humor.

When you're feeling out of control perhaps the last thing you want to do is laugh, but it can help.

One woman in Maryland, named Carol, wasn't laughing the night her doorbell rang and her nephew's "date" showed up. "This woman looked like she was almost my age," Carol said, adding, "which is about 15 years older than Jim (the nephew)."

For a minute, Carol tried to convince herself that this stranger had the wrong address. "Then Jim ran downstairs and they started slapping five. I couldn't believe it," Carol said. Knowing that discouraging her nephew from dating someone would probably make the attraction stronger, Carol offered this "older woman" a glass of lemonade and then excused herself from the room to get it.

"It gave me time to recover," Carol said. "And I needed the time.

I made the lemonade from scratch." Carol did what I often suggest to adults in situations like this. Not only did she stall for time by jumping into a famliar routine for a moment so she could calm down and collect herself, but she tried to remember when she was her nephew's age and brought home boyfriends.

"There was the boy whose hair was longer than mine, and my dad thought he was a girl," Carol said. She obviously remembered that teenagers often assert their independence from the family by choosing the very people their parents find objectionable. By the time Carol came out of the kitchen she was smiling. "It was a ridiculous situation," Carol said. "Ten years before, this woman could have been babysitting for my nephew at fifty cents an hour. And here she was, dating him. I told myself that it had to be better that she looked more like Mary Poppins in a leather vest, than Jack the Ripper. Heck, I just let them go."

Jim returned home safely, by the way, and after a few more of these dates, he soon turned to someone Carol found more suitable. If you ask me, Carol's sense of humor saved the day.

8. Model the traits you'd like to see in a youngster, such as patience, tolerance, good manners, and social responsibility: This involves putting ourselves where our mouths are. Consider all the traits you'd like to see in your teenager. Is caring about those less fortunate at the top of your list? There are programs to volunteer for, loads to be made lighter. Hopefully, you can find something that you and your teenager enjoy doing together.

I was so heartened, recently, to hear about one young man, Kristopher, in Southern California, who after years of working and volunteering beside his dad, had organized a group of his fellow college students, during their spring break, to build homes for the impoverished in Tijuana.

For all the traits you hope to see in your teenager, set a good example. If you'd like to see patience, then learn to be patient.

One teenager recently wrote a message to me hoping that I would share it with parents. "Remember," she wrote, "whatever we see you doing, we're almost bound to follow behind in the same footsteps."

I couldn't have said it any better myself.

9. Provide for interaction. This goes beyond watching a television show together. The idea is for youngsters to learn to feel comfortable talking to adults and other elders.

Board games rank at the top of the list for providing interaction in successful families. One woman told me of a "stupid" game she and her family played over and over for years. They laughed and groaned together at their mistakes. Unlike watching television, these games provide an opportunity for participants to talk and chatter. You might try several games before you stumble upon one that everyone in the family enjoys. The idea is that youngsters learn to talk to adults without feeling intimidated. Go out and find your fame, sport, or activity, and have some fun.

10. Help your youngster develop a game plan for life. There's another kind of game I often refer to, and that's the game of life. Successful parents teach their children that they must have the right equipment if they want to reach their goals.

One mother, Anne, a really good woman in Washington, D.C., and her husband have three children. Their first daughter attended college for six years and finally dropped out without ever getting a degree. She now lives on public assistance. The son followed his first sister's path pretty closely. After a few years in college, he decided it wasn't for him either, and he, too, dropped out. His mother went to visit him recently, where he works as a bouncer at a "topless-bottomless" bar. Then, there was the youngest child. She seemed to be the brains in the family. She went on to college then, after two years, also dropped out. She's now employed as a clerk at a department store.

I know this mother gave her children "everything," including love, patience, and a fine home. I also know that not everyone is cut out for college. So we have to ask ourselves what happened here. College tuition is expensive, but not as expensive as the disappointment this woman and her husband have to be feeling.

There is only one ingredient that may have been missing in this family, a game plan. Let's assume that not one of these kids was suited for college. That's something that could have been determined earlier on, so alternate plans could have been made.

There are hundreds of professional schools and technical institutions. Surely they'd have had something to offer at least one of these kids. Sometimes, when we can't find the answer ourselves, we must turn to a professional career counselor or school guidance counselor. Whatever you do, remember not to try and foist your dreams on your children. Give them the freedom to decide what they want to do, then help draw up a plan about how to achieve it.

Teach them that it's important to look at life as a game. The rules and fundamentals are based upon the knowledge we gain. The players include family members, society, and peers. There are also the boundaries of protocol and manners. Stress that there are time limits to getting things done, tools and plays to use. There is even a mental play book, which requires savvy to understand how to stay on top. Without a game plan life can be a losing proposition.

11. Refrain from giving ultimatums.

When you were a kid, did you ever draw a line on the sidewalk or in a sandbox, and dare another kid to cross it? Well that's what some parents do with their teenagers. Take my advice. Leave the ultimatums to the kids. All we can do is tell them what we believe in and state firmly what we would rather they not do.

Schools of Parenting—
What Works, What Doesn't?

Ultimatums are generally tactics employed by parents who endorse what I like to call the "T.O.B. Institute of Parenting." T.O.B. stands for Ton of Bricks. This philosophy emphasizes absolute and total control. The motto is "When I say move, you move. When I say jump, you say how high." If a child doesn't do what she is told to do, the philosophy is to come down on her like a ton of bricks. The belief system is that people are basically evil and must be controlled.

This T.O.B. style served its function when life was hostile and demanding: frontier life, for instance, or during any period when the work world demanded children who obeyed and followed orders. In those times, people rarely questioned authority, and punishment worked well. Parents said it. The children accepted it, and that settled it, no questions asked.

One drawback of this school of thought in today's society is that victims of threats and ultimatums look for ways to strike back and get revenge. Parents who attempt to exercise absolute control are likely to promote rebellious behavior. Even if the child appears to be an absolute angel when growing up, he will often rebel in adulthood or feel deeply resentful.

Of course, parents should not go to the other extreme, either. Which brings us to the second school of parenting, the "O.O. Honey College of Parenting." These parents are really not sure what they stand for. They just want everybody to be happy and not worry. Their motto is "I'm sure he can make it if we just let him do his thing." Whatever a child wants is fine in this school—it doesn't matter when, where, or how. Just "don't have a cow, man."

WARNING: This school is also linked to extreme reactions and behavior. Many youngsters want limits. The world can be frightening without them. I know one young man whose mother usually responded to his requests by saying, "Go ahead. I don't care."

Then one day her son called her on it. He said, "I want you to care."

The third and final school of parenting is the one Nichele was raised in. It is the "I.M. Reasoner School of Life." This democratic school maintains that life itself is the greatest university of all. It acknowledges the presence of challenges and the perplexities of choices and consequences in all human endeavors. Its motto is "Life is a gift, don't trash it." Its philosophy states that "Without discipline, there is no freedom. Democracy requires diligence, cooperation, and decision making." It acknowledges that freedom has limits, and children are encouraged to discover, and within certain parameters, take risks and learn. They are given age appropriate opportunities and encouraged to be responsible.

12. Pay attention and give attention. Remember that every child is unique. What works with one may not work with another. Know your teen and the setting in which he or she is attempting to thrive. Take nothing for granted. Praise and encourage your teen. Promote family activities.

Central to this school's commitment is the strengthening and development of character by teaching and modeling values.

If you hope to be successful as a parent, it's important to look closely at your school of thought and consider changing it. You'll find that starting a new habit—12 of them in fact—only *sounds* frightening. Once you begin to put them to work, you'll be heartened by the positive response from your youngster.

You'll want to get started right away by looking closely at our first step, "letting go," which, as promised, is discussed in detail in the next chapter.

Summary For
Successful Parenting

Summarized below are the attitudes and actions that successful parents employ to effectively communicate with their teens.

1. **Relinquish control of minor issues.**
   Learn to let go of the little, everyday things that don't matter much in the larger picture.

2. **Look deeper than the "headline" news.**
   Look beyond your youngster's outlandish behavior and/or appearance and try to get to its source. No matter what, let her know that you love her unconditionally.

3. **Listen.**
   Allow your teenager to express himself so that you can understand his motivations and feelings. Remain calm. Doing so will open the doors to better communication.

4. **Incorporate personal narratives into casual conversations. Pass down family lore.**
   The two activities are integral to maintaining a good relationship with your youngster. He will gain a sense of you, and your history—in other words, the real human being who sometimes masquerades as "The Parent." Family lore will impart values and a connectedness that have the ability to sustain your teen throughout life. Lore can be valuable for dealing with moral dilemmas and other types of conflict.

5. **Maintain rituals.**
   To develop a sense of security and family, rituals are important. Rituals can take any form, from yearly family picnics, to jogging with one another, once a month. Consistent family interaction fosters love, care, and security in your young adult.

6. **Admit fallibility.**
   If a mistake you made affects your teen detrimentally, then you must offer him a heartfelt apology.

7. **Maintain a sense of humor.**
   Laughter can alleviate tension and anger.

8. Model Traits.

Set an example for your youngster by behaving respectfully. If it is your desire that your daughter grow up to be socially conscious, then you must involve yourself in some humanitarian activity. It is helpful to become active in an area that is of interest to your teen so that you can share the experience.

9. Provide Interaction.

Board games are an excellent means towards interaction and open communication. Teenagers can learn to interact with adults, and not feel intimidated, and vice versa.

10. Help your youngster devise a game plan for life.

To do this, you must first find out what your teen's interests are. From there, the plan and strategy can be mapped out to insure success in just about any endeavor. All the love and communication in the world could be wasted if your son has no goals or aspirations.

11. Refrain from giving ultimatums.

Explain the consequences of your daughter's actions, instead. Ultimatums can often backfire and cause rebellion in your teenager. Your best bet is to allow your child to exercise a certain degree of independent decision making. Democracy in a household is key to developing and maintaining family ties. It is also essential to building confidence in your daughter.

12. Pay attention and give attention.

Note how you respond to your teen and how he responds to life's challenges. Your child needs you to be there.

What Teens Say:
Common Battlegrounds

We offered teenagers a multiple choice quiz of eleven possible areas of conflict, and asked them which, if any, their parents complain about. Of 469 students;

241 listed their bedrooms
239 listed chores
 85 listed homework and grades

They Said Their
Parents Also Complain That:

- "I waste too much time."
- "I'm always in my room and not with them when I'm at home."
- "I want to control my own life."
- "I worry too much."
- "I'm greedy."
- "I'm too spoiled."
- "I'm too self-centered."
- "I'm too wild."
- "I have a trusting vulnerability."
- "I have a sick sense of humor."
- "I hate my dad's music."
- "I'm rebelling."
- "I don't tell them everything."
- "I push their limits."
- "I find fault too easily."
- "I have a Porsche brain and drive it like a VW Bug."
- "I'm a slob."
- "I refuse to acknowledge their opinions."
- "I'm insecure."
- "I talk too much."
- "I fight with my sister."
- "I'm disorganized."
- "I talk on the phone too much."
- "I'm forgetful."

- "I have a very bad temper."
- "I fight with my brothers."
- "I procrastinate."
- "I am not blindly obedient."
- "I stay out too late."
- "My mom doesn't like my hairstyle."
- "I'm always asking for money."
- "I don't try hard enough."
- "I don't open up to them."
- "I defend myself."
- "I don't listen to them."
- "I'm not good enough for them."
- "I'm always asking to go somewhere, never home."
- "I spread myself too thin."
- "I don't do enough."
- "I try to take on too much."
- "I'm lazy."
- "I'm not responsible."
- "I criticize their stupidity about their divorce."
- "I participate in too many activities."
- "I don't show my mother respect."
- "I'm not motivated."
- "I don't realize how good I've got it."
- "I'm lazy at home and work hard at school."
- "I don't speak their native language."
- "I argue with my mom."
- "I don't make my bed."
- "I get defensive easily."
- "I want freedom."
- "I don't take anything seriously."
- "I dump my problems on them."
- "I roll my eyes and make faces at them."
- "I'm dishonest."
- "I'm sometimes inarticulate."
- "I'm not very affectionate."
- "I don't follow directions."
- "I am a perfectionist."
- "I don't know what to do on my own."
- "I'm a grouch."
- "I'm not as prejudiced as they are."
- "I think of myself first."

- "I disagree with them."
- "I'm always sad when I talk to them (mostly my dad)."
- "I'm too open."
- "I can't accept it when they say no."
- "I have an ability to make a mess wherever I go."
- "I'm too pushy."
- "I'm a picky eater."
- "I yell too much."
- "Pick the wrong friends."
- "I act stupid too much."
- "I am sensitive."
- "I don't work hard enough on physical jobs, like stacking wood."
- "I am sometimes too negative."
- "I eat too much."
- "I have a snotty attitude."
- "I talk too fast."
- "I watch too much TV."
- "I am too loud and outgoing."
- "I'm too busy for family stuff."
- "I'm too impatient."
- "I am scatter-brained."
- "I'm moody."

8

What You Can Begin To Do Now

There's an old joke about a man who was always telling his son to tuck in his shirt. Every time he saw the boy he nagged him about it. Then one day the boy walked into the room with his shirt tucked in. His father took one look at him, paused, then said, "Tie your shoelaces."

A lot of adults believe that to be effective parents they must have absolute control over their children. Few things could be farther from the truth. Parents who overcontrol are burdensome, annoying, and smothering. They are also parents not listened to by their youngsters. Their children see them as prison guards about to issue one more warning about yet another rule.

Letting Go

On the other hand, there are effective parents. They let go, even when it hurts. They learn to isolate that which is of utmost importance and let go of that which is not. I know this is easier said than done.

My two-year old daughter, Lindsay, means the world to me and my wife, Karen. Evenings, when we return from work, we rush to wrap our daughter in our arms. No matter how difficult the day has been, embracing Lindsay and holding her tightly in the circle of our love seems to reduce all the world's problems to mere backdrops in the human drama. I'm certain that, as a parent, you've experienced these feelings. And that means you have also known the feelings of ambivalence when you watch your child take his first steps without you.

You felt pride because those unsteady steps signalled to the world that you had nurtured your child and given him the strength and self-confidence to walk unaided. But you must have felt frightened, too. Those same steps also meant this child, whom you hold so dear, was now also capable of walking away from you.

Those conflicting feelings remain with parents all throughout life, as our children grow and begin to travel even more freely in the world. But just as we are expected to let go of their tiny hands, we must learn to release our teenagers.

Letting go means allowing a youngster to choose what he wears or how he will keep his room or even whether he participates in a family prayer ritual—as difficult as it may be for you, and him.

Choose Your Battles

I'm not suggesting that you just give up on your child's religious education, (if you've made religion part of your lives), or that you stop insisting he keep his room clean. I am suggesting that you choose your battles wisely. That's the first step in letting go. Keep in mind that this is an important part of the communication process. If you want to be heard by your teenager, you must decide what is of utmost importance to you, and let the others go.

You can begin this very necessary chore by making out a list of all the actions that cause friction between you and your teenager. Put them all down—the big, the bad, and the ugly. Your list could include everything from doing homework with the radio on, to smoking cigarettes, to leaving the top off of the toothpaste.

Making a List and Checking It Twice

Try and remember that no one has to see this list but you. Don't bother to mince words. Here's one woman's list about her daughter.

1. is boy crazy
2. monopolizes the telephone
3. keeps messy room

4. doesn't work hard enough in school
5. is rude to her stepfather
6. watches too much television
7. doesn't finish chores
8. eats too much junk food
9. doesn't write thank you notes
10. isn't polite when answering phone
11. wears a ridiculous hair style
12. puts ketchup on everything I cook
13. plays music too loudly
14. procrastinates
15. argues with me about everything

You'll probably agree that this is not an unusual list of complaints. Compare it to your own, and as your eyes scan this page of obnoxious behaviors, try and imagine your child changing completely. Poof! Just like magic, he has been transformed into: The Kid Who Does Everything Right. He never complains, he rushes to do your bidding, even sets the table for dinner, after, of course, finishing up all his homework from his honors math class . . . Difficult to picture, isn't it? It might even be impossible to imagine loving this kid, and for good reason.

He's not your child. He's the kid from across the street, and while he's pretty nice, you don't love him. You do love your child, though, warts and all. Soon, you're missing your kid and you realize all his behavior that drove you crazy was part and parcel of who he was—from quirky personality traits, like his interest in snakes and rodents, or his aesthetic preferences, to that loud rap music, your child is unique.

The Importance of Letting Go

If you try to force your youngster to goose step behind you into adulthood, you're sure to be met with either resistance, rebellion and shutting down, or someone who is robbed of creativity, spontaneity, and a zest for life. I know you don't want that, so let's look at how you can let go safely, and offer your teenager a sense of freedom in his life. Let's also say goodbye to those parental myths we hold so dear, which include:

1. I can direct every turn of my child's life.
2. I must protect my child at all costs.

3. I have control over other people's lives.
4. It is my responsibility to look for solutions.

It may be just as important to understand why we resist letting go before we can begin to. One woman who has done a lot of thinking about this subject is Oakland, California's Dr. Lorraine Bonner, a Stanford University trained general practitioner, who has a 15-year-old daughter and an 18-year-old son.

As her children have matured and insisted on their right to be independent beings, Dr. Bonner has observed her own "letting go" process with the eyes of a scientist and the heart of a mother.

When I asked her to share some of her observations with us for this book, she wrote a letter theorizing why we adults have difficulty shifting gears as our youngsters get older. She said many parenting styles are dependent on the simple notion that grown ups are bigger than their kids. When our children were little, for instance, and the time came for them to go to bed, or for someone to decide what they would wear, "we took it for granted that we were supposed to exert power over them," Dr. Bonner said.

When they become teenagers we continue to hold on, abusing that authority, and using that "power in self-serving ways," Dr. Bonner said, "especially so we can feel in control of situations." That's where the problem lies, Dr. Bonner continued. "If you feel in control of your teenager, something is dreadfully wrong with the way you're raising him."

She said, "Sometimes everything inside a teenager feels confused and out of control—maybe a lot of the time. They, of course, broadcast this (as all of us broadcast our inner feelings), and we grown ups pick up on this and it touches our own buried, confused, and out-of-control feelings.

"In an effort to calm ourselves," she continued, "we quite naturally try to clamp down on the source of discomfort, but it doesn't get us what we want. In fact, it may produce quite the opposite effect.

We have to accept the realities: If living an unpredictable life makes you feel out of control, you will feel out of control if you live with a teenager. And if your life with a teenager is not unpredictable, you have done something that may be detrimental to his or her emotional health."

Dr. Bonner said teenagers are supposed to separate and establish their own identities. "This is their developmental task," she wrote. "It's even more important than mowing the lawn or washing the dishes (but just barely). My research has generated the following hypothesis: the way teens sometimes separate is by establishing, in their minds, whatever it is that makes you who you are, and then they do the opposite."

It may not be the stuff for a scientific journal, but I think up to a point Dr. Bonner is correct. With her thoughts in mind, reread the list of your teenager's obnoxious behaviors. It's time to get clear about what is *Really Important*. If your teenager engages in life threatening behavior, it's Really Important that he not do so. On the other hand, the kind of clothes he wears, or what he does with his hair probably isn't. The more you narrow your list down, the easier it will become to communicate. If you try to exert too much control about relatively small issues, your teenager will become so resentful that when you try to talk about what really matters he simply won't hear you.

The Importance of Holding On

To continue paring away at your list, you might want to glance through Chapter Four again to ascertain how your own core issues influence your need to control your child. After doing this, you'll probably be left with about five or six Really Important issues. For instance, depending on who you are and what you believe, you may well insist that attending religious services is just as important as doing well in school.

You are bound to have subjects that you're unwilling to compromise on, and that's just fine. These reflect your character and individualize your home. But promise yourself that once you've reduced your list, you'll continue to be open to dropping more issues as your teenager matures.

Except for the Really Important Issues—taking drugs and drinking head this list—you'll want to give some of the smaller, more debatable subjects, such as hairstyles, choice of music and friends, a lot of thought.

There's a method for doing this, which I introduced to one woman, in Seattle, whom I shall call Diana. She refused to budge on the subject of her 14-year-old son Karl's room. I thought Diana's experiences would be of particular interest to you, because in my surveying of teenagers, the subject of their parents complaining about their sloppy rooms turned up more often than any other.

When I asked Diana why she insisted that her son keep his room clean, she just shrugged, as if I should already know the answer. "Well, obviously I want him to know how to be a neat human being so he can survive in this world. I want him to be able to get along with other people. Neatness is expected, and the place where we learn to be neat is in our home."

"That sounds good to me," I said. "But what do you think the real reason is?" "That's it," Diana insisted. "Knowing how to be neat is part of living in a civilized society." As I stared at her she began to squirm. "What," she demanded. "What are you thinking?"

"Are you suggesting that he won't be civilized when he grows up, if he doesn't learn to clean his room?" I asked.

"Of course not," Diana said, "but it's also embarrassing when people come to my house and his room looks like a pig pen."

I had a feeling we were getting a little closer to the truth. "Why can't you close the door and just tell visitors it's your son's room and he'd prefer that they not go in?"

She allowed that she could do that but insisted again that she couldn't let him live like a slob. I asked her what approaches she'd been using and for how long. She said that, in the last eight years, she'd scolded, nagged, lectured, punished him, and, when all else failed, cleaned his room herself.

"Has it worked?" I asked. Diana nodded her head yes, but looked unsure. "Oh," I said, "You mean that once he cleans his room he keeps it clean?"

She looked at me as if I'd lost my mind. "Follow me," she said, and led me to Karl's room. I was unprepared for what I saw. Christmas had been celebrated months before, but a string of colored lights lay forgotten on the floor, alongside comic books, discarded tissues, heaps of clothing, candy papers, a scattering of shells from sunflower seeds, and caseless Nintendo cartridges. Also, the bed was unmade, the sheets filthy, and the desk was covered with video and audio tapes.

I turned to her. "So," I said, "this is the result of eight years of scoldings . . . Do you really believe your method has worked?"

Diana said she was ready to try something different. I made some suggestions about what she might do, which began with asking herself some questions. I've listed them below because I believe they can help you pare your list down. Try answering the following questions:

1. What is the problem? What does your child do or not do that causes friction between you?
2. What approaches have you used to bring about change?

3. Why do you insist upon this behavioral change? Is it perhaps life threatening, endangering his future or morally offensive?
4. What is it that you ultimately hope to get from your child by insisting that he change? Is it love, respect, obedience?
5. Is it logical to believe this approach will give you the results you're hoping for?
6. Why do you think it hasn't worked?
7. If you admit it hasn't worked, ask yourself why you've continued to use it anyway. Look at your own behavior carefully and try to understand what benefit you've derived from it.
8. What are you feeling about this subject now? Are you frustrated? Furious? Determined to try something new?
9. Having thought about this, what is your goal now?
10. What is your plan for reaching that goal?

Among other things, Diana said she wanted her son to learn how to get along with other people and not to be looked down upon by those who might consider him sloppy. She said she believed that one day he'd thank her for teaching him the virtue of cleanliness. But she said she certainly didn't feel any gratitude now. As a matter of fact, she admitted, it had become like some spiteful game they played. She'd scream at her son, telling him to clean his room, and he'd spend an entire day doing so, dragging out each step, as she nagged and coached from the sidelines. Then by that night, his room would begin getting messy again.

As for what she'd gotten out of it, forcing him to clean his room did make her feel she had some control over her son's chaos. Finally, she said she was willing to let go. She was tired of putting so much energy and ill-will into something that was ineffective. In fact, at my prompting, she estimated that over the years she'd spent at least an hour a week (if not more) scolding her son about his room. That added up, over a period of eight years, to 384 hours of scoldings. That's ten full-time weeks of work. Consider how different her relationship with her son might have been if she'd spent ten weeks really conversing with him.

Relinquishing Control and Assigning Responsibility

As question number ten suggests, Diana devised a plan. She decided on a bottom line for her son's room, had a long talk with him, and began keeping a diary detailing her new approach, as well as her son's response. Here's some of what she later told me.

First she got her husband to agree to go along with her. Then she told her son she wanted to talk to him and they scheduled a meeting. When that time came she told him that she didn't feel like nagging him about his room anymore. "You aren't me are you?" she said. "When I was a kid my room was always clean and my mother never had to ask me to clean it. But it's not fair to expect you to do just what I did. Somehow, somewhere, I learned that it's important to have order in life, that it seems to make things go more smoothly. I have to hope that will happen to you. I'm proud of the person you've become. I know you're mature enough to take care of your own things and I'm going to let you start doing that."

She gave Karl permission to take control by saying, "It's your room. You are now solely responsible for it."

She then outlined natural consequences:

1. You must keep your door closed when your room is messy. When it is clean you may keep the door open. If you leave the door open and the room is a mess, it won't matter where you are, what you're doing, whether you've got company, are on the phone, or in the middle of dinner. You must stop and clean the room.
2. I will not walk into your room when it is messy, and that includes delivering laundry. I will place your freshly cleaned clothes outside your door and if you do not take them inside after seeing them, I will pack them away for future use.
3. If any of your homework papers are lost in your room because of the messiness, then that's a problem you'll have to deal with.
4. If you eat food in the room, the cups, dishes, or any leftover food must be disposed of, immediately, because they might attract bugs. If that is not done, then once again, you must clean your room and will, from that point, be forbidden to take food into the room.

When she was finished, she said Karl looked at her in disbelief. "You mean all I have to do is keep the door closed and I can keep it any way I like?" She reminded him of the other guidelines, then assured him he'd heard her correctly.

She then asked him if he preferred a written contract or a verbal one. He chose the latter. "That's fine," she told him. "I trust you."

A month passed and it was a long one for Diana. The few times she did see the inside of her son's room, as he passed in and out, she had to bite her lip to force herself not to say anything. "It looked like he was trying to grow some alien bacteria in there," she said. "Once when I was talking to him at the door, a strong smell emanated from the room. It was not a pleasant experience."

He did test her as I told her he would. When she came home from work one day, his door was wide open. "He was lying on the floor watching television. I asked him to clean his room. He said he had to study for a final exam and I didn't want to keep him from doing so, but a deal is a deal. We'd made an agreement and I thought it was more important to adhere to it." On day 32 of the experiment, she phoned me with good news. When I answered, she didn't take the time to identify herself. I heard her say, "He cleaned it. He actually cleaned it. I can't believe it. It's amazing."

I don't have to tell you how ecstatic she was. "The feeling of having him do that on is own is incredible," she said. When she'd asked him why he decided to clean it, he said he just couldn't stand it anymore.

Her success encouraged her to stop controlling him in other areas also. He'd been arguing with her about attending Boy Scout meetings. He hadn't wanted to join, but she'd insisted. She now told him she'd prefer for him to go and explained why, but added that it was up to him. He quit. He also asked if he could stop attending his Saturday afternoon algebra tutoring class. She said yes, but that since it was his weakest subject, she asked that he do extra math homework on the weekends. She also cautioned that if his math grades began to slip, they'd have to reconsider the decision.

Drawing the Line

I wish I could say all their squabbling came to an end. But this is real life we're talking about. His parents hadn't changed all the rules. They were still against R-rated movies. They told him so. But a week later, he went to a theater and saw one anyway. Diana and her husband were discouraged.

When they confronted their son, he didn't deny it, and complained, "You guys don't let me do anything. I'm the only kid who has to go to baby movies."

Diana pointed out that in recent weeks they'd granted him many privileges. But she stuck to her guns. This R-rated movie rule was one they wouldn't bend on. She and her husband, John, discussed some of the recent studies that explained how kids are negatively impacted by watching violent movies and television shows.

Their son still resisted and said he was tired of being treated like a baby. John told his son a story about when he'd felt the same way. I'd like to share that with you.

"When I was 15, Steve was my best friend, and his brother, who was in college, got a new car that Christmas. It was British, a Rover, supposedly the safest car on the road. And that New Year's Eve, Steve's brother invited us both out to a frat party with him. It was the first time he'd offered to take us along. He'd always said we were babies."

"But my folks said I couldn't go, that I was too young. I tell you, when Steve and his brother left that night without me, I felt like the world had ended. I would have sneaked out of the house and gone with them if I could have gotten away with it. "

"It wasn't until the next morning that I heard the news. They'd gotten into an accident, but the advertisers had been right. Steve and his brother walked away from the crash. The car did sustain a great deal of damage, though, and when I went to see it, I just stood there gawking. The front seat of the car was intact, but the back seat had been crushed, and that was just where I would have been sitting. I didn't feel grateful to my parents at the time and I sure didn't connect my being alive with them not letting me go. They said 'no' about a lot of things, some that I still disagree with them on. But they had been right about that night; I wasn't supposed to be in that car.

"The problem with being on two sides of an issue, the way we are now about these movies, is that when their kids are safe, parents don't always have something dramatic, like a wrecked car, to prove they're right. That makes it harder to say no, but when it concerns your well being, we have to say it anyway."

John and Diana offered to watch one of these movies with their son, for the sake of the discussion. That night, they rented "Robo Cop II," the son's choice.

Diana said she and her husband sat silently through several of the most violent scenes. Halfway through the movie, the boy turned off the television, rewound the tape and handed it to John. "Maybe we can talk about it again in a couple of years," he said.

When they asked him why he'd given up on the idea, he said that when he watched the movie with them, he could see it through their eyes, and that when he grew up he wouldn't let his kids watch something like that either. He apologized for having gone to the other R-rated movie and promised he wouldn't do it again.

"I was very proud of him," Diana said.

I was proud of the way John and Diana had handled the problem. They made some hard decisions about letting go, and with all the superfluous nagging pushed aside, their son was able to hear them when they discussed what was Really Important to them. And they talked without nagging, just the facts, which included a report on violence, backed up by a personal narrative from John.

I must say, though, the fact that Karl didn't lie when they confronted him made their job a lot easier. When parents are faced with a bold-faced lie it's hard not to fly off the handle. The first thing we usually feel when it happens is the need to get them to tell the truth, at all costs.

Letting Go of Lies

One man, a dentist whom I'll call Jack, told me recently how he'd just dropped Jason, his 16-year-old son, off at a bus stop. They'd been arguing about the amount of the boy's allowance, and he said his son was surly and kept complaining that his life was miserable, that he'd never been so unhappy in his life. The boy didn't say goodbye when he got out of the car, just slammed the door.

This man was upset and was thinking about the unhappiness his son had expressed. So it wasn't until he was on the freeway that he realized he was going in the wrong direction. He drove back onto the street and happened to pass his son. The boy was still waiting for the bus but seemed to have undergone a personality transplant.

"He was holding court," the father said. "He was standing in the middle of the crowd making everyone laugh. He was the life of the party. That was the first time I realized why he was so popular." But that's not what made this dentist so angry with his son. He also noticed that the boy was smoking. "I wanted to run him over," Jack said. "No wonder he was always broke. Cigarettes are expensive, not to mention the fact that they might kill him."

He calmed himself and kept on driving. That night, as soon as he arrived home from the office, he began upbraiding the boy for smoking cigarettes. Right on the spot his son said, "When you saw me, where was the cigarette?"

His father paused for a moment. "Why, it was in your hand."

"Then that explains it," said the boy. "You saw me when I was holding a cigarette for my friend. I wasn't smoking."

Jack tried to get his son to admit the truth, but to no avail. Jason could have held his own in a prisoner of war camp. He wouldn't admit anything.

How often we find ourselves in a similar situation. We know our kids are lying and they know we know it, but they persist. They can come up with a lie faster than we can say "you're grounded." There's only one solution, and it's the same that I gave you at the beginning of the chapter. Let go. Forcing the truth out of them is a means of control, and, as Dr. Bonner said, an abuse of authority. It doesn't do anyone any good.

Meanwhile, if you're absolutely certain that you're correct, and he is lying, tell him you're having difficulty believing him. Ignore his lies and proceed with what you think is best. Try to remember, though, that consequences always work better than punishments. In the case of the dentist and his son, I think Jason should be required to take one of the smoking clinics sponsored by local hospitals.

He'd be certain to hear enough from his fellow attendees about why he should put a stop to this terrible habit before it becomes an addiction. This way, the boy is allowed to think through the situation, and is given the sense that he controls his own future by acting responsibly now.

Next, we'll see how letting go is an important part of creating resilient youngsters. You can guide your teenager into a maturity that allows him or her to withstand the toughest peer pressures.

What Teens Say:
"This is the Advice We'd Love
To Give Our Parents . . ."
(Psst, Mom and Dad . . . Read This)

(Each phrase or sentence represents a new voice.)

- "Listen as well as you speak."
- "Don't fire questions at teenagers because it's frustrating."
- "Support your future leaders."
- "Please do not act like you know everything."
- "Have patience, we're going through a hard time in our lives and sometimes you make it worse."
- "Relax, we aren't going to bite your head off so don't treat us like aliens."
- "Don't nag."
- "Sit back until you're really needed—we can take care of ourselves."
- "Pack away your pride."
- "Give us space."
- "Trust us."
- "Remember that teenagers are neither stupid nor ignorant and our opinions are as valid as any adult's."
- "Remember how hard it was."
- "Try to decipher messages out of what we say."
- "Let us have some fun."
- "Look at yourself before you get on your kids' back."
- "There is no right way, every kid is different so try to wing it."
- "Children would not lie or be dishonest if they did not feel forced to."
- "Listen as well as you hear."
- "Spend a year in high school with me."
- "Go to a parents' conference and learn about what we're really like."
- "Take us seriously and don't belittle us—we are capable."
- "Give us time and we will succeed."
- "Give us a chance to fail."
- "Stop yelling all the time because we can hear you if you talk low—it's not helping anything by yelling."

- "Stay calm."
- "Make a pact with your kid."
- "Realize we have social lives too—and don't always expect us to have everything done by the time you get home."
- "Remember you were a teenager and not a perfect one."
- "Give us a chance to talk."
- "Don't try to be a teenager because you are not."
- "Don't think of us as kids but people."
- "If you treat teenagers like children we'll act like children."
- "Don't make quick judgements about teenagers because not all of us are pregnant druggies."
- "Be cool."
- "Don't make conversations as long as a book."
- "Be yourself."
- "Talk *with* them, not *down* to them."
- "Have a long temper and a short memory."
- "Make sure you let them know you love them."
- "Don't stereotype teenagers—open your eyes."
- "Let us make our own small decisions."
- "Be more of a friend than a warden."
- "Be straightforward, up front, and open—say when you're just having a bad day."
- "Try to understand we have a lot to deal with."
- "Treat us the way you would have liked to have been treated when you were a teenager."
- "Adults should try to build friendships with teenagers by talking with them all the time about everything, not just when there's a problem."
- "Don't act like a teenager or pretend to be one."
- "Let us be ourselves."
- "When punishing us, don't ground us for long periods (like a year); a little while will do."
- "Remember that the times have changed."
- "Try to remember that you were in our position too."
- "Listen with an open mind."
- "Respect us as complete people."
- "Support our dreams."
- "Give us a chance."
- "Tell it like it is."
- "Don't be a stereotype."

- "Treat us like adults except when we are in mental or physical danger."
- "Remember that sometimes we just want to be left alone."
- "Give us a little room to grow."
- "Step back and let us make our own mistakes so we'll know how to correct them later on."
- "Never ask the same questions twice."
- "Be a little understanding before you start yelling."
- "Be honest and we will communicate more if we know you're not lying to us."
- "Speak calmly and rationally."
- "Understand the whole situation before you point fingers."
- "Be more perceptive about a teenager's emotions."
- "Treat us like the educated individuals we are."
- "Try to compromise so both of us are somewhat happy."
- "Don't pose as an authority figure."
- "Have a discussion not a lecture."
- "Adults must realize that teenagers are subject to many things that parents, during their day, may not have experienced."
- "Don't fight us, join us."
- "Don't judge us by exterior appearances—keep an open mind."
- "Don't always push your company or advice on us."
- "Don't be condescending."
- "Have passion."
- "Stop yelling—geez."
- "Understand that teenagers honestly think they know everything but they don't."
- "Treat them as equals, and you'll get honesty, but treat them as inferiors, and you shall get dishonesty."
- "Always be there to answer any of their questions."
- "Relax."
- "Remember, you were young and foolish once too."
- "Give them the benefit of the doubt—there are two sides to every story."
- "Teens just want to be liberated like anybody else and they deserve that."
- "Don't hold back!!"
- "Listen, truly listen."
- "Read a book about teenagers."
- "Try to keep up with current issues facing teens—remember that teens have changed and you have to change with them."

- "When you say something, stick to it."
- "Listen to us—because some of us are really smart."
- "Talk everything out, it makes for a better family situation."
- "Be open, everything unexpressed is just a hindrance to your relationship."
- "Be emotional and not always professional."
- "Put yourself in my shoes and try to imagine how you'd react to what you're doing and telling me."
- "Adults shouldn't say they know just what it's like because times have changed."
- "Be more understanding and forgiving . . . you'll get a lot further in life."
- "Understand we are yearning to explore everything and we want it all."
- "Remember we do have views that are truly ours."
- "Don't ask us about every little detail."
- "Never make a subject off limits—anything should go."
- "Be a good example."
- "Never FORCE a close relationship."
- "Treat teenagers as you would want them to respond."
- "Stop being repressive."
- "Don't get mad."
- "Get out of the '50s and '60s and get into the '90s."
- "Trust that we can hold our own in a corrupting environment."
- "Let go."
- "Remember you are talking to people, not just teenagers."
- "Ask us, don't tell us to do something—we usually won't refuse."
- "Make the punishment fit the crime."
- "Listen and don't prejudge."
- "If you're patient you will have no problem."

III

MOVING
TOWARD
NEW LIVES

9

Creating Resilient Teenagers

A few years ago, I heard from a former classmate who, with her husband and 17-year-old daughter, had moved across the country to accept a high ranking White House position. As this woman talked about the impact of the relocation on her family, I asked her permission to take notes. I'd heard no story more convincing than her daughter's, of the importance of raising resilient teenagers.

The Anatomy of a Decision

I'm going to share this girl's story with you, making certain to include all the vivid details. That way, when we examine the events leading up to the crucial moments, you'll know them well enough to freeze-frame them in your mind. This is not an intellectual exercise, but an attempt to understand why some youngsters give into negative peer pressure and others resist it.

According to my former classmate, once her family made the move to Washington, it took almost no time for her husband to settle in. He's an attorney and his firm readily accommodated him with a job transfer. But the move did prove to be hard on their daughter, whom I shall call Helene.

Cross country moves are highly stressful for any family, but consider this girl's circumstances. An only child, she had been born and raised in the same small town, had attended neighborhood parochial schools, and was part of a group of best friends whom she'd known since kindergarten. Now here she was, ready to start her senior year in high school and forced to leave the only life she had ever known.

Not surprisingly, Helene was angry with her parents. She even asked them to allow her to remain in her hometown to live with an elderly aunt. Her parents quickly nixed that idea. The aunt was old and infirm. Also, they felt that since a youngster's senior year is fraught with transitions and life impacting decisions, they wanted to be there with her.

That parental mandate sent Helene into a long, drawn-out state of melancholy. There she was, as the family looked at prospective homes, wandering in and out of rooms, her eyes downcast and distressed, the embodiment of adolescent gloom, as if she had been asked to choose her own mausoleum.

Their old house sold quickly, and at a good profit, so they were soon able to buy a new place in a prestigious neighborhood.

Meanwhile, Helene was filled with apprehension. What would her senior year be like? Would she make new friends? Would the other kids laugh at her for being from a small town? She felt unsure of herself in this sophisticated milieu.

She insisted on attending a school that her parents believed was thoroughly wrong for her. Still, they gave in. It was part of a negotiated settlement. They agreed that if she cooperated with the move, they would allow her to make the final decision about her school. It was an institution that would have intimidated most kids, for it was filled with the progeny of the Capitol's powerbrokers. Only in this school, the youngsters ruled the day. Instead of the old plaid and blue uniforms Helene had always worn, she was now expected to wear the latest fashions, as well as have a car of her own. Some of the kids were dropped off in limousines that transported their famous parents to the Hill. Other students drove BMWs and Jeeps.

Helene lobbied for a car of her own. Her parents called a family meeting to discuss it. Helene argued that if she went to a driving school she could get her license in a few weeks. Her parents were willing to negotiate, but only to an extent. No car they said, until she had taken a driver's ed course, and practiced defensive driving for several months with a licensed driver. They backed this up with some statistics they'd read on teenage drivers involved in traffic accidents. As for the car, they added, they, too, felt she was responsible enough for one of her own. But they were not willing to buy it for her. She would have to get a summer job that next year, earn the down-payment, and they would handle the monthly installments, if she paid her own insurance costs.

Helene got hysterical over this. She couldn't wait until next year, she said, everyone drove except her. She hated them, she said. Of all the parents in the world, how did she get them? She rushed off to her room. By the next day, though, she seemed to have forgotten about the car and didn't mention it again.

After a few weeks at school, she probably realized that the differences between herself and these new kids went far beyond modes of transportation. These new girls at her school spoke freely about the sexual liaisons they'd had. She was still a virgin. Many of them had experience with liquor and marijuana. Helene had only tasted wine on Sundays at communion. Her classmates took to calling her the nun, because they said, when it came to fun, Helene didn't "give nun, or want nun." It became the campus joke, and she hated it almost as much as her new life.

Sometimes her parents wondered if they'd made the right decision about the move. Helene was having such a hard time adjusting. They had to put in long days on their new jobs, and that meant even less time to spend with her. After a few weeks, though, they agreed that one of them had to be there most evenings with their daughter. Often, they took turns. On one occasion that meant the mother had to say no to an emergency meeting with the Chief Executive.

They were a busy couple, but they found ways to spend time together. No matter how angry or noncommunicative Helene was, the one family ritual they continued was Sunday evening dinners of hamburgers and strawberry shakes. Helene had made the shakes since she was big enough to press the blender buttons. Her dad barbecued the burgers, even during the winter. They got a kick out of watching him set up a grill in the snow, as he moved about in his insulated boots, and down jacket. They called him the Michelin Tire Chef.

It wasn't as if Helene seemed to appreciate any of this, though. She usually acted as if her parents didn't exist, seldom initiated a conversation, and only answered their questions in monosyllables. They tried talking to her anyway.

Sometimes that meant they only said hello, asked her how her day had gone, and they always reminded her that they loved her and wanted to listen to her, whenever she was ready to talk. Her general response was to go to her room and slam the door.

In the meantime, at school, Helene was trying desperately to fit in. Once she tried smoking a cigarette in front of some of her classmates, but she choked so badly, it only gave them more to laugh about.

After the first term, her grades plummeted to Cs. Her parents called another family meeting. They told Helene they understood her unhappiness about the move. The father talked about a major change he'd had to undergo in his life, when he was 14, when his father had lost his job at a factory. "Our whole life changed," her father told her, "but I was still expected to keep going just as if it hadn't. Life is filled with changes."

They told her they expected her to work as hard at this school as she always had, despite their change of address. If not, they added, she might fail one of her classes. And the consequence would be attending summer school, rather than working at the part-time job. Helene's response? Well, these days all their family meetings seemed to end in the same manner: She rushed off to her room, saying they would never understand her, and slammed the door.

By the spring term, her grades picked up, and her moods began to vary. One some days—depending on something as unpredictable as a break in the bad weather, or a smile from an attractive boy, or a long letter from one of her best friends back home—Helene seemed positively ebullient. Other days she'd mope about the house like a stalk of limp celery.

She became obsessed over the senior prom. What would she do if no one invited her? Everyone else had a date already. Then out of the blue, it seemed, she was graced with an invitation. Even better, the fellow who did the inviting was handsome and popular. They'd been in the same biology class. Carl, as I shall call him, had just broken up with his long-time girlfriend (who was already dating someone else).

As the prom date neared, Helene's mother took her shopping and Helene chose a dress that was a knock off of one she'd seen her favorite actress, Jodie Foster, wearing at a televised Academy Awards presentation.

On the night of the gala Carl arrived on time, driving his father's sleek roadster, with another teenage couple waiting in the back seat. Carl was handsome and mannerly, Helene's parents noted. He presented their daughter with a corsage and they posed for the obligatory photographs. Then, after being grilled by her parents on the details of the after-party, the two were off. Everything worked out splendidly for Helene, at the dance. Carl was an attentive escort, other boys begged her for a dance, and "everyone" complimented her on her dress.

Winning Values

About midnight, the most popular kids, including Helene and Carl and the couple riding along with them, piled into cars and headed for a nearby lake, where there was moonlight and music—supplied by some boom boxes—and long, uninterrupted talks about college plans and life in general. It must have all seemed so grown up, so sophisticated.

When someone handed Helene a cup of beer—the kegs had seemed to materialize almost miraculously—she simply said no, and the styrofoam cup was passed along. She'd given drinking a lot of thought and felt perfectly comfortable saying no. But as the evening progressed, and it got to be two, three a.m., she noticed her date was belting down one beer after the next. When she mentioned this, he said not to worry, that he'd been drinking for years and could handle his liquor, and that this was only beer, anyway. But she was not comforted. She noticed Carl was slurring his words and that when he walked to a nearby bathroom, he stumbled.

What was she to do? She was 35 miles from home, so she couldn't walk, and she didn't know any of the others well enough to ask for a ride. Besides, the others appeared inebriated also. The best course of action, she reasoned, was to just keep quiet, not draw any attention to herself, and try to enjoy the remainder of the night.

Finally, the other kids started leaving. Like Helene, most had promised their parents they'd be home by dawn. As she and Carl headed for the car, Helene noticed that he, as well as the other couple, sounded "out of it." Well, what of it, she thought. Parents always talk about the kids who do have accidents when they're drunk. What about the ones who get home safely? Grown ups were always exaggerating.

As Carl put his arm around her, it warmed her to think about the upcoming summer, when she hoped to be invited to more parties, and maybe even by this young man. Then she could go to college and hang his photo on her wall. What a coup. As if reading her thoughts, Carl began telling Helene how much he liked her and she moved in closer for reassurance.

She was frightened by his unsteadiness, though. As they walked on, she spotted what might ultimately be her salvation. It was a coin phone and she had a quarter in her purse. Her mother always insisted she have extra money when she was out. She wanted to telephone her parents, tell them where she was, and ask them to please come and get her.

She knew calling them would mean an end to everything, her new friends, Carl, summer dates. He was sure to call her a dork, she thought. She felt lost. Her thoughts and actions seemed reduced to singular moments. Her feet moved ahead . . . They passed the phone . . . Past Safety . . . Into the parking lot . . . Some cars pulled out . . . Shouted goodbyes . . . Engines roaring . . . Carl unlocked the trunk and put the blanket in. He unlocked the passenger door, the others piled in. Her turn, and then a voice, "Get in Helene." It was Carl.

She froze. "I can't" she blurted. "You've had too much beer. I'll call my parents. They'll pick us up."

Just as she'd predicted, the other couple began laughing. Carl grabbed her arm, she hadn't counted on that. He looked incredulous, furious, his mouth tight, then sagging, when he let out air. "You can't do this," he shouted, and he looked bigger than she remembered. "If my parents find out I've been drinking again, I'll be grounded."

She stood firm. "Please let go of my arm," she said, but he kept tugging at her. Would he drag her into the car? Then the other girl called out, "Just leave that stupid bitch here. She's a little girl."

Carl pushed Helene away. "You're right," he said. They were in the car and pulled away almost immediately, leaving Helene, in her Jodie Foster gown. The sun was coming up in this long, deserted expanse of parking lot. She didn't even know if the phone was in working order. Luckily for her it was, and when she heard her father's voice she began sobbing. "Hurry up," she shouted, "this is all your fault."

After her parents had picked her up and she'd slept several hours, they had a family meeting. First they told her how proud they were of her decision, then asked the tough question. "What do you think we should do," her mother said.

"About what?" Helene asked.

"About the other kids?"

"What do you mean?" Helene asked.

"They were drinking," her father said. "They put their lives in danger. Shouldn't their parents be told?"

Helene began crying.

"No, no. I couldn't do that. I mean, they must have gotten home without an accident. We haven't heard anything. That would make it even worse for me. Please don't do that."

Her parents said they understood that she wouldn't want to be embarrassed any further, but they added that something did have to be done about the others, that it was their responsibility as adults, to do something. They asked her to think about the most appropriate measures.

Two days later they came up with a plan and they put it into action. The mother visited the school principal (without her daughter), explained what happened, and asked him, if possible, to refrain from identifying Helene. He addressed the senior class about the incident and sent letters to all parents, handling it as a school-wide problem, and leaving it up to the parents to determine the extent of their youngsters' involvement. A psychologist, who specialized in drug and alcohol abuse, was called in to lead workshops.

As for Helene, while the word did get around that she was the catalyst for all this activity, she wasn't treated like a social pariah. Everyone seemed preoccupied with graduation. She never did make any solid friendships that summer but she survived.

Today, she is a student at a major university, where she hopes to follow in her father's footsteps and study law. At the moment, she says she'll "just die" if she doesn't get chosen for the summer internship she's applied for. So we leave her anxious but settled.

When I looked through my mental file of remarkable youngsters, I realized I could have told you about any number of teenage heroes. There's the kid who risked his life to rush into a burning house to save an old man. There's one who stood up to a neighborhood drug lord. Another reported her marijuana-smoking parents to the authorities.

But not one of them could have made a point better than Helene. Her dilemma, on that moonlit night at the lake, was a common one, and lacks the drama of a made-for-television movie. She simply chose not to drink or ride with someone who had. It may not be earth-shaking, but it's the kind of split-second decision-making our youngsters are faced with daily.

What we usually realize, and they usually do not, is that their choices can make the difference between whether they live or die, fail or succeed, or begin a path on which retreat is virtually impossible.

Think: What personal stroy can you offer that involves a good or bad decision you made in the face of peer pressure?

The Typical Teenager,
Counting the Ways

I had another good reason for choosing Helene. Those other heroes—
the kid in the fire, etc.—would have sounded like earthbound gods.
Our kids are flesh and blood, and tend to be much more like Helene.
It's not that your youngster can't be an exception, but I think Helene
was a pretty typical teenager. Let me count the ways.

1. Teenagers experience the same emotions as adults, only more
   intensely. Helene's moods changed as quickly as the weather. One
   minute she was sulking, clammed up, or arrogant. The next she
   seemed cheerful, optimistic, and talkative.
2. She viewed herself as the victim of her parents' whims and felt they
   didn't understand her.
3. She wanted desperately to fit into her peer group and be considered
   "cool," that is, nonchalant and fashionable. (Of course the standards vary from group to group. What might be cool for a suburban
   cheerleader would not be the same for an urban gang leader.)
4. She felt inferior to other kids, and her sense of self was tied to how
   she was perceived by her peers.
5. She (usually) believed that her parents' fears were greatly exaggerated.
6. She had a need to establish a separate identity from her parents.
   (Although Helene's folks attended Catholic schools up to and
   including undergraduate school, she broke with tradition by insisting on a nonsectarian institution for her senior year and college.)
7. She masked her anger. Rather than talking to her parents about her
   feelings, she acted out by slamming doors and throwing temper
   tantrums.
8. She worried about being attractive, strong, respected and intelligent
   in the eyes of her peers.

The list doesn't end with Helene, though. Compared to the way
adults live their lives, teenagers tend to be forgetful, unreliable, and
impractical, particularly as their actions relate to the future. And when
it comes to something they really want to do that we don't approve of,
they sometimes think it's worth the risk of getting punished.

I'm not trying to give teenagers a bad name. I believe that if you can accept the objective reality you can be a better parent. Of course it would make the job a lot easier if youngsters followed all our rules, listened carefully when we scolded or lectured, and behaved more consistently and responsibly.

But if that were the case we'd be talking about a new natural order. And if we're going to dream of that, let's not stop with teenagers. I've got a friend who is a deep sea diver. Life would be a lot easier for him if he could just jump into the ocean, knowing that all the sharks out there were friendly and would never attack humans.

And I'm looking forward to taking my daughter, Lindsay, to the circus, one day, to see those daring highwire performers in action. They live with the reality that one misstep might send them plummeting to the ground. Wouldn't it be great though, if after falling, they could land softly and with grace? But those are only dreams. The reality is that some sharks will attack humans, and that if we fall several dozen feet there's a good chance we won't walk away to talk about it. It's called the law of gravity. It's unfair but that's the reality these people must keep in mind if they want to succeed at what they do, whether it's deep sea diving or balancing on a wire.

It's the same for parents. It behooves us to understand the nature of the adolescent. I believe Helene's parents knew what to expect from their teenager, and in their awareness, were able to create in her a remarkable resiliency. They gave Helene a strength that allowed her, in that dark and near empty parking lot, to claim her life as her own. As much as she may have wanted to ride with the others, she held firm to her beliefs. As much as she wanted acceptance and popularity and independence, none of it was enough to make her follow along, as the others piled into their cars, jeopardizing their lives.

Why Many Parents Succeed

What did her folks do to create this resiliency? Well, let's take a look at their parenting style. I think it speaks volumes.

1. They were parents who kept communicating even when their daughter resisted speaking. Although Helene was only answering them in monosyllables, they didn't try to force her out of her tight-lipped funk. She was entitled to her feelings. They let her know they cared about how she was doing, and were willing to listen to her problems. Their action could be interpreted as saying, "We care about you and love you."

2. They established principles for Helene to live by. She must have put a real damper on their new life in Washington, and it certainly would have been easier to leave her in the old hometown, but they didn't. They said they expected her senior year—a year that prepares for transitions—would be a tough one for Helene emotionally, and they wanted to be there for her. They insisted, despite Helene's anger, that their family belonged together, not thousands of miles apart.

Also, they believed they would rob their daughter of a sense of accomplishment if they simply purchased a car for her. They agreed to help her out, by paying monthly car notes. First, they told her, she had to work and earn the downpayment as well as the money for the insurance.

3. They were willing to negotiate with Helene, and did so within the context of family meetings. These meetings send a clear message: "We're all in this together."

As is the case in most negotiations, neither party got everything it wanted. For example, Helene's parents disagreed with her choice of schools, but accepting her choice was part of their bargain.

4. Also, as relates to the choice of school, they seemed cognizant of her need to separate from them. The mother and father had both read books and taken workshops on what to expect from their teenager. They were prepared.

5. They knew their daughter was unhappy over the move but they were not alarmed by her behavior, and did not turn to someone else for help. They knew what danger signals to look for. These include the following traits:

a) A youngster who has no faith in either his own, or the world's, future. Someone who is nihilistic, that is, who shows a total rejection of your moral beliefs and principles (such as skin-heads, who proudly wear Nazi swatzikas). Or a youngster who threatens suicide (no matter how casual that threat may seem).

b) A kid who is generally a loner, and who is forced by peers to remain on the outside.

c) One who suffers long, uninterrupted depressions.

d) A youngster who acts out of control, getting into clashes with authorities, uses drugs, or drinks.

e) One whose school functioning drops dramatically and without justifiable cause.

Although they kept a close eye on Helene for these signs, they were relieved when she displayed none of them.

6. Rather than punish, they explained consequences. They were concerned about Helene's grades but rather than threaten her with extremes, they reminded her she might have to spend the summer making up grades rather than saving money for a car. When you punish a child harshly or unfairly it can easily be interpreted as a hostile lashing out, and the youngster is left with the feeling that she wants to "get back at you," even if it means that she'll get hurt herself.

7. They set guidelines and limits for Helene to live by. They were comfortable with her driving but only after a period of safety instruction.

8. They told her about their concerns and backed them up with irrefutable realities. They discussed the dangers of drinking and driving, shared the alarming statistics about teenagers involved in auto fatalities, and then let her go. They had to be a bit frightened about Helene driving off until dawn, with a boy they'd never met before, but they didn't nag her or lecture her about their fears. They showed trust in their daughter's judgement.

9. They understood that their daughter's sense of identity would, in large part, be affected by her dominant peer group. Although Helene did not become part of the "crowd" at her new school, she'd had the constancy of friendships back in her hometown with the group of girls who attended parochial schools with her. Their values were, to a large extent, shaped by the religious community they were raised in. But it might have been one of several groups, including scouting, summer camps, ROTC, 4H groups, hobby groups, ALA-TEEN, or any organization that builds leadership, self-esteem, or encourages camaraderie.

10. Helene spent time with a youth group that used role playing as a teaching method. Role playing is like a dry run in the theater of life. Certain situations are set up and participants discuss how they would react. It can be helpful during stressful moments if youngsters have been given an opportunity to think ahead of how they want to emerge from a situation.

Teaching Your Youngster To Say No

A lot of role playing is set up to teach basic refusal skills. Kids are taught to memorize key phrases for difficult times with peers. For instance, a teenager is taught not to feel uncomfortable asking another teenager hard questions about a plan that sounds dangerous. I've included those questions here:

- "Why do you want to go there (————use the friend's name)?"
- "What do you plan to do when we get there?" (keeping your voice calm.)"
- "Listen to me, do you realize how much trouble we could get into?"
- (Pause.)
- "Would you like to do ————, instead?"
- "If you decide you want to be with me instead, I'll be. . . ."

This method is best learned within the safety of a peer group with a qualified leader. It tends to be too contrived between a parent and a teenager. When our kids are with us, of course they are going to say what they think we want to hear.

Now, onto the final strategy used by Helene's parents.

11. Helene's parents made time for her, even at the expense of their careers. Although most of us don't have as many hours to devote to our youngsters as to our work (and they wouldn't want us to either) it is important to make our children priorities in our lives.

While no method is foolproof, I believe these 11 strategies will increase your probability of raising a teenager with strong positive character, someone who can withstand the tough but ordinary challenges of adolescence.

In the next chapter we'll take a look at parents who must guide their youngsters with one voice. This not only includes mothers and fathers who have lost a spouse through divorce or death, but those whose mates are often away from the home due to job demands. But even if you do have a traditional marriage, you may find chapter nine to be one of the most important sections in the book, especially if you have a tumultuous relationship with your teenager.

10

One Voice

One of the most sweeping social changes in our world has been the divorce rate. About half the teenagers I meet come from single parent households, and that figure represents the nation as a whole. Fifty percent of the marriages in this country end in divorce. And missing from that figure, are the many households where one partner's preoccupation with work forces the other partner to shoulder the day-to-day responsibilities of parenting. I know there are a lot of you out there.

What's a Parent To Do?

Whatever your status—married with a busy spouse, or single, divorced, separated or widowed—if you're raising a child without consistent input from a mate, this chapter may prove vital to your peace of mind. You will learn communication skills you can hone and put to work immediately. My first priority is to help you understand that you are not disadvantaged. Don't laugh. That's just how one woman I recently met described being a single parent. She told me that life with her 15-year-old son had become impossible since her husband had moved out because the boy had no one to fear.

That's nonsense. Effective parenting doesn't rely on brute strength or fear. One adult who communicates from the head and heart is ten times more powerful than two adults who rule by intimidation.

If you are alone, however, you must face the reality that our society is not geared up to support and encourage parenting in general and single parenting in particular. If you work outside of the home, you're probably up early, running here and there, trying to make ends meet, without the benefit of trusting, fully available people. At the same time, all the mandates to perform as a good parent and to conform to your own standards remain in effect, just as if you had a spouse to lend emotional support.

There must be days when you feel as if you're in the middle of a circus performance. Not in the stands, but dead center in a three-ring act. In one circle, the clowns are making faces and blowing horns at a man-eating lion. In another, someone has been shot from a cannon, and he flies past you. And there you are, the juggler, trying to concentrate and keep those balls in the air, while a trained dog snaps at the seat of your pants.

That's just the way a lot of single parents feel. There's so much going on that you're afraid to even stop and breathe. And if you continue like this . . . maybe you can't. Why, just look above you. Who's that swinging wildly from the trapeze? It's the star of this show and he looks vaguely familiar.

Why, it's your teenager! One minute he's idealizing the missing parent, and furious with you; the next he arches back, spins in the air, does a flip flop, and now, he's enamored with you, disgusted by the other parent. Finally, he's trapped, in mid-air, caught between the two of you.

No wonder you feel dazed. You've been in the middle of an emotional balancing act. But look behind you, there's an exit.

The door opens to a clear path of peace, if you can learn to firmly and decisively:

1. Set emotional limits (managing how much of yourself you invest in what may be your child's problems. It's part of letting go).
2. Model "detachment" in non-life threatening situations that arise from the teen's own negligence. Allow natural consequences to take place.
3. Encourage grieving over the loss of a parent.
4. Acknowledge the realities of your lives.
5. Avoid unfair comparisons ("Why can't you be like . . .").

Divorces and Other Permanent and Temporary Separations

The best way to show you these five skills in action is to introduce you to the Stelly family of Phoenix, Arizona. They have survived a decade-long "separation" that ultimately ended in divorce for the parents. There are three children, including eight-year-old twin boys, and the oldest, Heather, now 16. The father has always traveled extensively for business. In fact, his former wife, Elaine, estimates that he is on the road 90 percent of the year. "For the last 10 years we just pretended we had a marriage," Elaine said. "At the time, the illusion of a marriage was all I thought I deserved."

I appreciate Elaine's candor about her marriage. It's important to note here that when parents "pretend" to be in a relationship that is good when it is not, everyone in that household is pulled into the lie. It teaches the children to be dishonest and causes conflicting emotions. They both love and hate their parents. The years leading up to Elaine's divorce are equally as important for us to understand. As in many marriages, they left the occupants of this house in quiet turmoil. To youngsters, it can feel like living in a war zone. So if their behavior sometimes seems bizarre, why should that surprise us? When it comes to a youngster's emotional well being, parental anger and rage, even when camouflaged, are just as destructive as mortar and shells to the emotional psyche.

The Stellys: One Family's Story

The divorce in the Stelly household didn't occur until the oldest child, Heather, was 15. The wife, Elaine, said, "We had some good times together, but often, when my husband and I were together, there was coldness and tension between us. He'd come in criticizing the way I was running the family, and he was constantly on my daughter about things . . . Her room was too messy, her teeth didn't look clean. The twins weren't reading well enough. The lawn wasn't being watered adequately. My kids would come home and ask, 'Will Daddy be home tonight?' I think they were relieved when I said no."

With the marriage in tatters, the oldest child, Heather, became, as some psychologists call it, parentified. That is, she tried to become the other adult in the family.

"She'd argue with my husband in ways I was afraid to," Elaine said. "She'd say things to him like, 'How could you not come home for Thanksgiving? This is so unfair to us.' And my husband and I would scold her for being fresh. We teamed up to silence and shame her."

As you can tell, Elaine realizes it was wrong to shame her daughter into silence. The truth is that Heather was right on target. She had a story in her mind that contained a vision of a family being together, especially on a holiday like Thanksgiving. That was not to be, and she was hurt, disappointed, and rightfully angry.

It may be true that, in terms of protocol and decorum, Heather brought up the subject in an inappropriate way. That's to be expected from a child. She simply didn't know better. However, the parents lost a golden opportunity to acknowledge her feelings and teach her a more appropriate way of getting her message across. Shame is a terrible weapon that parents can wield. It rips through genuine communication like a sword through a heart. Let's return to Elaine's story and learn more about Heather and her family.

"When she was 12 years old, Heather asked me why I didn't divorce her father," Elaine said.

"I couldn't believe she was saying that. I told her how blessed she was to have a father who worked so hard. That was the year I made her stand with me at the door to greet family members for our reunion. We have the showcase house in our family, our relatives jokingly bicker over who gets to spend the night. I wanted her to hear their compliments, to convince her I was right."

By the time she was 13, Heather began talking back to her mother. "I couldn't discuss anything with her. She'd blow up at a moment's notice," Elaine said. "Once I tried to take her television away from her and she locked herself in her room. My husband had to come home and threaten to break down the door."

Heather's response of "talking back" to her mother was natural and predictable. She saw her mother caught in a bind. It's not unusual for one marriage partner to tolerate a variety of aberrations, indiscretions, and abuses to avoid financial hardship or loneliness. But Heather was angry about her parents' marriage. Her insightfulness and sense of propriety caused her to rebel against her mother's inability to confront the husband and to face up to the looming possibility of having to end the good life.

Since Heather was reprimanded for her honesty, she responded the way so many youngsters do. She "got back" at the adults in her life by dressing and acting out in ways that infuriated them. According to Elaine, Heather began wearing seductive clothing, including very tight short skirts, jeans with large gaping holes positioned near her derriere, low cut midriff blouses, and one Easter Sunday, after spending the night at a girlfriend's house, she showed up at a family dinner with her hair bleached platinum, and wearing a black leather mini suit.

"She didn't wear a blouse beneath it, and there was only one button on the jacket," Elaine said. "It looked like her breasts were going to fall out. Worst of all, she wore a dog collar around her neck. My parents were so upset they couldn't get through the meal."

It wasn't until Elaine sought counseling for Heather that she owned up to the trouble in her own marriage. "Her therapist said that Heather had told her a story about a little girl. I can still remember it and it still gives me the chills. In this girl's bedroom there was a huge monster in the closet. The monster was vicious and loud but everyone in the house pretended they didn't hear any of the monster's noises or smell any of his excrement. I didn't have to be Freud to know she was describing my marriage."

Heather's counselor convinced Elaine to get help for herself and to work on her relationship with her husband. About a year into therapy, when Elaine began making demands on her husband, such as insisting that he spend more time with the family, he announced that he was divorcing Elaine and that he planned to remarry immediately, which he did.

"I was terrified," said Elaine, "Don't let anyone tell you that the money makes it easier. I thank God I wasn't left in poverty, but none of the things we'd amassed made it any easier for me to sleep at night or get through a day without sadness or humiliation. Everyone in my circle knew that my husband had left me for another woman. For a while I regretted having gone into therapy."

But when her gloom began to pass, she realized it was Heather who had been hit hardest by it all. "You'd have thought he was divorcing her," Elaine said.

Of course, in Heather's mind, her father was abandoning her. One does not simply divorce a spouse without precipitating feelings of loss and alienation in the children. The announcement of the divorce was like a death knell to Heather. To her, it spelled the end of hope. Like a lot of us, Heather seldom said what she meant. Although she had encouraged her mother to get a divorce, she was really saying she wanted her parents' relationship to change—for the better. It was like a cry for help. She was saying that she couldn't be happy unless they were.

What she was not prepared for was public acceptance of her parents' failure, the finalities of divorce, and her father's remarriage. Heather's behavior got out of control. "She began staying out late and hanging around with older men. Some were married," Elaine said. "I'd scare them away by threatening to call the police or their wives, but she'd always manage to find someone else."

When I met Elaine she was considering sending Heather away to a "school" for well-to-do troubled teenage girls. Elaine told me it would be best for them both. She admitted that sometimes she hated her daughter. I suggested that if she sent Heather away now, there was a good chance that when she returned from that school, she would have an angrier Heather, still acting out, but at legal age.

As we talked, I realized Elaine's decision might have been prompted by the fact that she had started dating another man. She said Heather was especially rude when this man visited. This, of course, is not an unusual situation, and I saw it as a place and time in their lives to begin making peace overtures. Elaine's beau happens to be a religious man who prays before each meal. Heather, who describes herself as an atheist, not only refused to join in with his prayers, but wore her radio headset to the table and turned her music up during the blessing. This was obviously distracting and usually ended with her mother screaming and insisting she leave the table. I told Elaine that while Heather certainly had the right to abstain from praying, her rudeness was unacceptable.

I suggested to Elaine that she have a long talk with her daughter before this man visited again. Her future goal would have to be setting limits and insisting on common courtesy from her, but that would all have to be saved for the future, I told her. Heather was already full of resentment because she'd been forced to live a lie for so many years. To salvage what was left of the relationship, I told Elaine she would have to "come clean," and break down the wall that separated them.

Ending the Chaos

I told Elaine that Heather is so perceptive that she had many choices about the kind of story she could tell her daughter. I asked her to try and sort out the most important points that needed to be made in her peace initiative. She listed the following subjects that she would want to discuss in her narrative:

a) Elaine's fear when Heather first began to speak up about the lies in their family
b) Her denial of Heather's feelings
c) What she wants now, with Heather, as she embarks on a new relationship.

I told Elaine that since personal narratives are so individual and spontaneous, it would be impossible for me or anyone to help write her script. But I offered her written guidelines with the following language:

1. Acknowledge the truth:
   - "Heather, I was wrong" And/or
   - "I've made some errors and as a result I blamed you for much of what was going on." And/or
   - "I probably haven't been very fair with you." And/or
   - "I know your father and I have made it very difficult for you in the past, and this new relationship of mine is not making it any easier now, is it?"
2. PAUSE, wait for some of this to soak in. This is, after all, a new and surprising openness. Whatever Heather's response, don't over react.
3. Acknowledge whatever is said. Look for and hear the feelings. If she's angry, or hurt, or sullen, acknowledge it. Look for one word that catches her feelings at the moment.
4. Apologize:
   "Heather, all I can do at this moment is to apologize and ask you to forgive me for the way I handled this. I can see that you were hurt by it and I can tell you haven't felt good about what's happening.
5. Wait. Take time with this and listen to her, even if she does not speak. Observe her body language. You did not hear her before so hear her now—including her body language.
6. Tell your story:
   - "Honey, I've got to tell you this has not been easy for me either. You know when your dad and I first moved here . . ." And
   - "When it all started to fall apart I felt . . ." And
   - "The point I'm trying to make is . . ." And
   - "But you were so honest . . ."

- "This is how I felt about the divorce. Did you have similar feelings?"

7. Be quiet. Let her respond. It may be silence, nonchalance, or discomfort.

8. Encourage her to speak. "How has it been for you lately?"

9. Listen.

10. Wave a white flag:
    - "I can't demand that you do as I say." And/or
    - "I can't supervise every decision you make." And/or
    - "There are some things I cannot stop you from doing."

11. Acknowledge the reality of your relationship:
    - "I guess there will always be times when we annoy one another." And/or
    - "The only thing we can do is try to figure out what's really happening."

12. Plan for future communication:
    - "Because things have really gotten out of hand with us I want to continue setting up times when we can talk."
    - "I like talking with you and I want to know what you think and feel about things."

13. Wait for response.

14. Don't wait for the bomb to drop. Be prepared for your own disappointment. The chances of a resentful and confused teenager suddenly opening up because you've made one attempt to come clean are minimal. Expect no immediate response for your efforts. Your only goal has been to put a crack in that wall, not blast it down.

15. Give it at least 24 hours to sink in. Don't bring up anything else for the moment. Time is required. She may test you to see if this is for real or not. At your next conversation ask her to do something with you that you both enjoyed in the past, and might enjoy now.

Of course I didn't expect Elaine to memorize these 15 guidelines for talking to Heather. She did read them over before making an appointment with her daughter. They met in Heather's room that night after dinner.

We open with Heather stretched out on a window seat as Elaine talks about the early years of her marriage. This passage may be particularly helpful for parents whose children resist full-scale conversations. Sometimes, if an adult continues talking to a troubled teenager, it can be like probing for the exact location of an injury. When you hit the sore spot, the child reacts, and lets you know you're on target.

A Dialogue

ELAINE: What would you think about us spending the weekend together painting your room?

HEATHER: Not if Dan helps. (Dan is Elaine's gentleman caller.)

ELAINE: That would be okay but later that day Dan might bring some Chinese food or something by. I'll probably be too tired to cook, and I enjoy being with him.

HEATHER: (Silence)

ELAINE: It's been so long since this room was painted. I can still remember when your Dad and I first found this house.

HEATHER: How old was I?

ELAINE: You must have been six, you'd just lost a tooth. We knew right away this would be your room. Remember that Victorian dollhouse we had in here?

HEATHER: Dad was supposed to put the lights in, but of course he was too busy.

ELAINE: The lights never really went on in our house either.

HEATHER: What do you mean?

ELAINE: It was kind of like we were all moving around in the dark. None of us knew how to be a family so we just moved through the motions the way you moved the dolls around in that house.

(Elaine is silent, as she waits for what she is saying to sink in.)

ELAINE: Whatever happened to those dolls and that house, anyway?

HEATHER: (Shrugs) Broken. It's in the closet, but don't go in there.

ELAINE: All of us are broken in a way.

HEATHER: Don't put me in this.

ELAINE: Then let's just look at me. I wanted so badly to fix everything, make our lives better, that was part of my brokenness. I thought that if I hung the copper pots in just the right place, and the towels matched, then it would really be a home.

HEATHER: It wasn't?

ELAINE: No, and you were the first to see that. You were like that little boy in the *Emperor's New Clothes*. The parade went by and you were on the sidelines protesting. You knew that the lights were out in our house, that we couldn't find each other. I heard you but I was afraid to tell you you were right.

HEATHER: (remains silent, but looks up at her Mom.)

ELAINE: I was just like you.

HEATHER: I'm not like you. You're beautiful.

ELAINE: When I was a girl, I was always trying to fix things for my parents, just the way you're trying to fix me and your dad.

HEATHER: How could I fix anything?

ELAINE: Think about it. What will happen if we keep having those scenes at the table when Dan is here?

HEATHER: I hate him, just like Dad.

ELAINE: But your dad isn't here, Dan is occasionally. So what could happen if Dan knows it's always going to be unpleasant when he comes?

HEATHER: I don't know. He'll stop coming. I won't have to watch him pick his teeth with a fork and . . .

ELAINE: Yes, he might stop coming by, at least that may be what you're trying to fix. Then maybe your dad will divorce his wife and he and I can . . .

HEATHER: That's ridiculous.

ELAINE: (Folding her arms across her chest) You're right. It is ridiculous, but not beyond the imagination.

HEATHER: I don't want Daddy back in this house. I hate him, I hate him. I hate Lorraine: (Stands and throws a pillow across the room). I wish they'd both drop dead. He's a liar and I bet he was sleeping with her all along. He made a fool out of you.

ELAINE: (faces daughter, continues in a calm voice) From now on, all those spiteful things you say about your father, tell him about them. If he's out of town, call Janet at the office. She always knows where to reach him. If you have to interrupt him in the middle of a meeting, that's up to the two of you. But I don't want your anger at him or Lorraine dumped on me anymore. This is the wrong address for it.

HEATHER: All you care about is Dan.

ELAINE: I care about you. I love you and I think you're very wise.

HEATHER: (Plopping back onto her stomach) Sure.

ELAINE: It's true. You know more than anybody else in this town.

You knew something was wrong with my marriage. It's not a relationship I'd want to go back to. The one you want to restore never existed.

HEATHER: Then you lied, too.

ELAINE: It may seem like that now, but it wasn't intentional. Do you know why I can see the truth now?

HEATHER: (angrily) No.

ELAINE: I stopped waiting for your father to turn the lights on in this house. I turned them on myself. And now I can see that nothing is the way I said it was.

HEATHER: (Buries her face in her arms and begins crying) Why can't it be? Everybody else has a family. Nobody else is like us.

ELAINE: Two broken people can't make a marriage. (She tries to stroke her daughter's hair, but the girl pushes her away.) I love you. And I am sorry for denying the truth all these years. I'm sorry you've had to suffer for us. But I have to tell you, I also want to have Dan in my life. Please don't try to fix things for me anymore. It won't work and it will only continue making you unhappy. I want you to be a part of our lives. I don't want you to go away to that school, but I want you to respect me, too. That means at least being polite to the man I want to be with.

(Elaine kneels down to Heather who is stretched across the window seat, with her head turned to the wall. Elaine points to a spot on the wall.)

ELAINE: When I look at this room, at the scotch tape on the walls, at the little piece of poster that never came off and the fingerprints, you know what?

HEATHER: What?

ELAINE: It doesn't look so bad anymore. With the lights on I think they look pretty good. The room looks real. You know what else I see?

HEATHER: What?

ELAINE: I have a daughter, who underneath the blonde hair and . . .

HEATHER: Ohhh please.

ELAINE: . . . And long red fingernails and spiked necklaces, is very beautiful but she's afraid to come out. She's not accustomed to the light. But that's okay, because I'm not afraid anymore and this time I'll be with her.

(She walks out and closes the door).

Elaine said that she and Heather did paint that room the next weekend, but Heather remained just as surly as she'd been. But there was difference. According to Elaine. "I felt better. It was almost as if I'd told the story for myself."

A week later she convinced Heather to go on a bicycle ride with her. They did and Heather, almost as if she were embarrassed, sheepishly asked Elaine, "Would you tell me some of those stories again, about when I was little." Elaine said it was the first time in years that she began to believe that things might work out between her and Heather.

It was just a beginning for Elaine and Heather, but as you can see they are off on firm footing, with Elaine leading the way toward peace. Most importantly, she acknowledged the realities of their lives. She and her husband did not have a happy marriage, just the facade of one.

Now that the air is somewhat cleared, she will have to begin setting limits with Heather about her behavior, particularly as it relates to Dan. She must steer clear of threats and offer consequences with regard to what is and is not acceptable behavior.

She must let Heather know that common human courtesy is a must in her home, or there will be consequences that could impact on Heather's relationships with her friends, including not being allowed to visit them, talk to them on the phone, or entertain them at her own home.

Heather's rudeness toward Dan was predictable. It was a power play. She was secretly saying, "Here you are bringing a new man into this house and we haven't even talked about the one who's gone. He's not my father and I don't have to respect either one of you." This was also Heather's way of redefining who she was and establishing her position as a key player in this "new" family.

Part of the solution to this problem with Dan is for Elaine and Dan to attempt to spend time with Heather, so they can get to know one another as a threesome, and so offhanded interaction can occur.

It's important to remember that people tend to reject or react negatively to someone they don't understand. Understanding comes through association, experience, and opportunities to be deeply involved in mutually satisfying activities.

Of course, acceptance may never occur, but they just might learn to tolerate one another. I told Elaine to allow Heather's relationship with Dan to take its course. In any case, she should remain available to talk to Heather about it.

Grieving Over the Loss
of a Parent

In upcoming months, as her relationship with Heather continues to grow, Elaine will have to build on her new foundation. She must lead her daughter through conversations about her dad that encourage her to grieve over him. Of course he's not dead, but the dream Heather had, that he become the head of their household, died when he left. A conversation that encourages a youngster to mourn the loss of your mate might begin this way:

1. How are you feeling about your father (or mother) being gone (or not calling, or showing up late, etc.)?
2. What do you miss most about not having him (or her) around?
3. What will you not miss?
4. This is what I remember most about him.

A parent must also learn to present the unbiased truths about a child's father or mother, no excuses. For instance, the wrong way would be, "Your mother is not here because she had to leave town suddenly for an emergency. I'm sure she wants to be with you."

The no excuses approach might be instead: "When I spoke to your mother on the phone she sounded as if she might be drinking again. I don't think she'll be here."

At the same time, be prepared to admit your part in the total picture. Every story has two sides. If your husband is a compulsive gambler, for instance, when you acknowledge this reality to your youngster, be prepared to tell how you fit into this picture. What issues and weaknesses are you also struggling with. "I take a lot of dangerous risks myself, and I've sometimes jeopardized. . . ." Elaine told her daughter she had a need to try and fix things, and that was part of her weakness. The need to control others is called co-dependency.

Remember, harsh criticism of your spouse only hurts your youngster. During adolescence youngsters are making choices about which parent they want to be like. If an adolescent is forced to be for or against a parent he is being robbed of freedom at a time when he most needs it. During this formative stage only your youngster can decide who he is. To do that he should be able to identify with you both, and that means he needs realistic pictures about both of his parents. So I urge you to remain evenhanded, as difficult as that may be. Let your child draw his own conclusions about which parent is right or wrong.

When your adolescent expresses angry feelings about the other parent, you can be supportive without being encouraging, by saying:

1. Tell me what hurts you the most about what he's done.
2. Has he done this before?
3. Let's look at your experiences with him.
4. What do you think you might do the next time this comes up?

This also means that you must avoid unfair comparisons. If you're feeling angry with your former spouse it's easy to hit your teenager over the head with it. How many times have you heard someone say, "You're just like your father," or "Your father did the same thing to me."

Even if you're feeling that way, this is one time to simply put a lid on it. Such spiteful and immature behavior, can damage a child's self esteem. You might say instead, "I've seen that same look in your dad's eyes. I wonder what it means."

Emotional Detachment

There's another tactic that's vital if you're to help your child survive when his parents lead separate lives. It's called emotional detachment and it is behavior that enables us to protect ourselves in hurtful situations. Remember:

1. You can't do for people what you want them to do for themselves. But you can set limits and shape an environment.
2. You should not create a crisis to effect a certain outcome.
3. You should refuse to cover up someone else's mistakes or misbehavior.
4. Do not let yourself be used and abused.

Finally, there's one more course of action that is almost a necessity for a single parent in today's world: support groups. They are helpful when you are with your spouse and twice as important when you're not. Members of these groups share parenting methods, information about community resources as well as advice and solace.

Nancy Macdonald, a brilliant family therapist in Seattle, Washington, whose advice was helpful in researching this chapter, has led a single parents support group for three years. She is often impressed with the wisdom and success stories she hears in the free, weekly meetings that she leads. She said single parents "need to know that they don't have to be alone."

In our resource guide, you'll find more information about how to locate a support group in your area. But first, I'd like to share some final thoughts with you.

11

An Open Letter to Parents

August, 1991

Dear *Reader:*

We've been on this journey for a while now, and my greatest hope is that I've offered you at least one idea that can make a difference in your life. I also hope the stories I've shared with you, as well as the step-by-step instructions on communication, will encourage you to rethink the way you relate to teenagers.

As you begin to share your personal narratives, remember that telling is not the same as teaching. Some parents get stuck on the telling part. They say, "All I have to do is tell that kid. . . ." Well, the truth is, some kids always seem to do what we expect, follow out rules and value what we value: others insist on having their own way and drive us insane. It's up to us to create stories so compelling they will be motivated in the right direction. Keep working at it, trying new approaches and techniques, until you've found the right words.

The rule is a simple one: *What works, works. What doesn't work, doesn't work.* Discard that which doesn't work for you. Keep that which does. It does no good at all to keep working hard at something that is ineffective.

If you've ever encountered someone who doesn't speak the same language as you, then you will understand what I mean by this. You ask this person something simple, say, for instance, "Where is the bathroom?" The person answers but in a language you do not understand. You're in a hurry, you've got to go. You repeat your question, but this time slowly. "Where-is-the-bathroom?" Once again, he tries to respond in his native tongue, but you interrupt, you're running out of patience. This time you not only speak slowly, but also enunciate: "Where . . . is . . . the . . . bathroom?" Again, the same answer: "###^*!!!!!" So now, you're screaming. "Where's the bathroom!" Give it up. It does no good to work at things that don't work. We know this and still that's what we do with our kids.

Take a look at yourself, for instance. Just because you know better, does it mean you do better? How many times have you given advice that you don't follow yourself? I can just hear you talking to a friend. "What you really need is to get organized." Then we go to your house . . . how many drawers do you have that you don't want opened? And what about that extra piece of cheesecake in the refrigerator? You've already had two slices. You tell yourself not to eat it. What do you do? You eat half.

Your youngster is no different. He wants to live life his way. So what are you going to do about it? That's right, you'll have to change if you want to motivate. I know it's going to be hard to change. That's part of the human condition. You don't want to let go. You've been doing it this way for so long. You're thinking, "Don't make me let go, it's too difficult." But let's make peace with our reality. Our kids are in trouble. If we're going to elevate their lives we've got to end the denial and face the realities.

We live in turbulent times—times that have swept us up in some of the most dynamic and intense changes ever known in the history of humankind. We have structured an environment that is unlike anything that man has ever known. And it seems as if much of the folklore and wisdom that serve to keep a culture intact and enable it to grow has not been passed down or developed yet. The knowledge needed by our youth is lagging far behind the growth rate of our high-tech society. So much is being forgotten that many of our children have no sense of how to negotiate success in the world we live in.

Have we failed to give them stories that put their lives in perspective, personal narratives that inspire passion? What messages are they given in a culture thrown into disarray? Our culture certainly hasn't had time to develop a response to all these changes. So our kids are responding on their own. They're doing the best they can. They develop according to the ideas they hold sacred, and they create stories and rituals and habits based upon these ideas. (Perhaps this explains the attractiveness of cults and gangs to some young people.)

What is sacred? It is clear to me that the development and advancement of any people depends on their having a strong sense of that which is sacred and important to them. In these times, I question what it is that we hold to be sacred. What are the things that we value? And what are the things we are telling our children? It is time for us to wake up. If it is indeed true that children are the future, then we need to invest in them as if our lives and well-being depended upon it. The future of this nation, and the world depends on our childrens development.

We're forced to ask, if they're only learning and talking to one another, what do they need us for? Well, as adults we can bring wisdom, maturity, and insight to help shape their perceptions. Sometimes we have to move them in the right direction while they're kicking and screaming. Wouldn't it be better if, when they hear our stories, they say, "Hey, I want to hear more about that," instead of absorbing so much of the folly of popular culture from television and the mass media.

Give your kids a chance. Let them learn from your pain, your resentments, your joys. Teach them that life is a gift, and that the greatest gift of all is their own mind. Arouse their passions, show them how to develop their skills and turn around and give some of it back to the world.

As a parent and concerned adult, stay alert to the fact that what we do makes an important statement to our teens. We must "be what we want to see. . . ." They need our example. Additionally, they need to know what it means to be a decent human being. They will learn from us as we:

1. Model patience.
2. Avoid using humiliation as a motivating force.
3. Share what we think is important, sacred and of value. Honesty, fairness, kindness, and forthrightness in the face of injustice or evil.

Our personal experiences. The experiences of others and the collective wisdom gained in maturity has enabled us to thrive and survive. Share it.

We have to help them understand that, in spite of the way the world is today, we still need them to play an active part in it. Let's get them fired up, to realize that each moment counts. From now on, every time you compliment your child, or encourage or support him, know that you're helping to shape his story. You'll know you're winning when you begin to see change.

Take every significant and necessary step along the way. When you hit an obstacle, stop and say, "Let's try something else. I believe in you." Let's rewrite those stories. Let's share our values and standards.

John Alston

P.S. Let me hear from you on the changes you see occurring.

RESOURCE GUIDE

WHO TO TURN TO WHEN
YOU NEED HELP

Following are a list of services that you or your teenager can turn to for help. Photocopy this list and make it readily available. It might be wise to read it thoroughly to familiarize yourself with what's available, so that you're prepared, if and when a problem occurs. All 800 numbers are toll free, and practically all agencies listed offer free services.

Abuse/Incest

NATIONAL CLEARINGHOUSE ON CHILD ABUSE AND NEGLECT —This agency offers information on child abuse and neglect. It provides referrals to local child abuse agencies. Call (703) 821-2086, or write, NCCAB, P.O. Box 1182, Washington, DC 20013.

NATIONAL CHILD ABUSE HOTLINE—This is a 24-hour referral service for prevention and treatment services. Counselors will also provide information and suggested reading material. Call (800) 422-4453.

PARENTS ANONYMOUS—This is a helpline so parents can air grievances with other adults. This service offers information on where you can find Parents Anonymous support groups, referrals to state chapters in 33 states, information on how to start a chapter, and referrals to other national resources. Call (800) 421-0353. 8A.M.—5P.M. PST. After these hours there may be either a machine or call forwarding.

Aids

NATIONAL TEEN AIDS HOTLINE—Referrals to the Good Samaritan Project. Call (816) 561-8784. Monday through Friday, 4–8p.m. CST.

THE NATIONAL AIDS HOTLINE—Provides confidential information in English and Spanish, referrals, and a brief recorded message.

Callers can also elect to speak to an information specialist to ask questions about AIDS or request free brochures.

Call (800) 342-AIDS.

Alcoholism

ALATEEN—This free program, with meetings held around the country, is one of the best of its kind. It is designed specifically for teenagers who have a parent, or any loved one, who abuses alcohol or drugs. For information on meetings in your area, check the local telephone directory for Alanon, or call the Alanon/Alateen hotline: (800) 356-9996, or write, Alanon Family Group Headquarters, Midtown Station, New York, NY, 10018-0862.

Also, local Alateen meetings pop up so frequently, that even the Alanon headquarters seems to have trouble keeping up with them. If they are unable to give you an Alateen schedule for your area, ask for the Alanon (adult program) schedule. You will find that by attending one of these meetings yourself, you will be able to get local information, from participants, on current Alateen meetings, or on how to get an Alateen group started in your area.

ALCOHOLICS ANONYMOUS—AA is the nation's largest self-help group for recovering alcoholics. Look in your local telephone directory under Alcoholics Anonymous, Alanon, or call this number: (212) 686-1100, weekdays, 9A.M.–5P.M., EST. They provide information on regional offices and pamphlets upon request. Mailing address: P.O. Box 459, Grand Central Station, New York, NY 10163

NATIONAL COUNCIL ON ALCOHOLISM AND DRUG DEPENDENCE —This is a referral agency which lists 200 state and local agencies on alcoholism. They provide telephone numbers and addresses, some with chapters specializing in self-help programs for teenagers who drink. Write, 12 West 21st Street, 7th Floor, New York, NY 10010, or call (800) NCA-CALL for general information.

ALCOHOL AND DRUG HELPLINE—24-hour hotline. Referral to alcohol and drug dependency units. Call (800) 821-4357.

NATIONAL CLEARINGHOUSE FOR ALCOHOL INFORMATION —This organization will provide you with free informational brochures and booklets in English and Spanish and referrals to local agencies specializing in alcoholism. Write, P.O. Box 2345, Rockville, MD 20852, or call (301) 468-2600. Hours are Monday through Friday, 9A.M.–7P.M. EST. There is also a helpline at (800) SAY-NO TO (Same hours as above).

Drugs

NATIONAL INSTITUTE ON DRUG ABUSE HOTLINE—Will answer basic drug questions and gives referrals to drug and alcohol treatment programs in your region. They will also send you free information brochures. Call (800) 622-HELP. Hours are Monday through Friday, 9A.M.–3A.M. EST. Saturday and Sunday, 12 noon–3A.M. EST.

COCAINE HELPLINE—24-hour referral service for local treatment programs, including counseling centers and support groups. Operated by the Psychiatric Institute of America. Call (800) COCAINE.

JUST SAY NO FOUNDATION—This operation offers information on starting or joining a local Just Say No club to prevent drug abuse. Call (800) 258–2766, or write, 1777 North California Boulevard, Suite 210, Walnut Creek, CA 94596-4112. Telephone hours are Monday through Friday, 7A.M.–5:30P.M. PST.

NATIONAL FEDERATION OF PARENTS FOR DRUG-FREE YOUTH (NFP)—Can direct callers to regional drug counseling services. Call (314) 968-1322. Hours are 8:30A.M.–5P.M. CST, Monday through Friday. P.O. Box 3878, St. Louis, Missouri, 63122.

Driving Dangerously

MOTHERS AGAINST DRUNK DRIVING (MADD)—24-hour hotline provides counseling, prevention techniques, victim hotline, literature, and nearest chapter referrals. Call (800) 438-6233.

STUDENTS AGAINST DRUNK DRIVING (SADD)—Same as above, but for teens. Call (508) 481-3568. Hours are 8A.M.–5P.M. EST.

AM I DRIVING SAFELY? BUMPER STICKERS—This is an idea originated by a teenager who was involved in speed-related accidents.

This bumper sticker is similar to the ones you've seen on the back of trucks. It advises readers to call the driver's parents if the teenager is seen driving perilously. They may be purchased for $2.00 each, or three for $5.00 by writing: Fred Stangle, P.O. Box 11633, Albuquerque, NM, 87192. Be sure to specify if you want the sticker to say: "Call My Mom" or "Call My Dad" or "Call My Parents." You add your phone number yourself.

Eating Disorders

OVEREATERS ANONYMOUS—Don't let the name fool you. This includes eating disorders of all kinds, including anorexia, bulimia. This referral hotline offers information for free and local meetings of Overeaters Anonymous, which can provide you with help for the family as well. Call (800) 873-8732, operates 24 hours, 7 days a week.

NATIONAL ASSOCIATION OF ANOREXIA NERVOSA AND RELATED DISORDERS—This organization helps anorexics, bulimics, and their families. It has chapters all over the nation, including Canada. It offers telephone crisis counseling, information, referrals, and self-help groups. Call (708) 831-3438, or write, ANAD, Box 7, Highland Park, IL 60035. Phone hours 9A.M.–5P.M. CST.

Family Problems

FAMILY SERVICE OF AMERICA—A referral service to 290 local agencies to assist individuals and families in solving parent-child problems, including tension, drug and alcohol abuse, teenage pregnancy, child abuse, support groups, etc. Counseling is provided with fees based on the person's ability to pay. Mailing address: 333 7th Avenue, 3rd Floor, New York, NY 10001. (212) 967-2740, Monday through Friday, 8A.M.–5p.m. EST.

Psychological Counseling

AMERICAN PSYCHOLOGICAL ASSOCIATION—This Washington-based organization can refer you to your local state association for the telephone number and address of a licensed psychologist. Call (202) 955-7600, or write, 1200–17th Street, N.W., Washington, DC 20036, or ask your school psychologist or counselor for a referral.

Pregnancy

PLANNED PARENTHOOD FEDERATION OF AMERICA, INC. —Provides counseling, information and pregnancy testing. Fees based on a person's ability to pay. Check your local telephone directory or call, (213) 541-7800, or write to the federation at 810 Seventh Avenue, New York, NY 10019. No telephone counseling. Hours are 8:30A.M.– 5P.M. EST.

Runaways

THE NATIONAL RUNAWAY SWITCHBOARD—24-hour crisis line. Arranges message deliveries for runaways who want to reach their parents or guardians. They also help locate shelter, food, medical help, and counseling for the runaway. Call (800) 621-4000.

RUNAWAY HOTLINE—Designed to help the runaway, arranges shelter, food, medical help and counseling. Call (800) 231-6946. In Texas, (800) 392-3352. These numbers provide message relay from runaway to parents.

Sexually Transmitted Diseases

NATIONAL SEXUALLY TRANSMITTED DISEASE HOTLINE —Answers questions about all sexually transmitted diseases, and makes referrals to treatment centers and hospitals and clinics. Call (800) 227-8922 or (800) 982-5883, weekdays, 8A.M.-11P.M., EST. After hours, there is an information message on dealing with symptoms and prevention.

Single Parenting

PARENTS WITHOUT PARTNERS—A national program with many local chapters, this organization sponsors support groups and offers information. Check your telephone directory or call (800) 637-7974, or write, 8807 Colesville Road, Silver Spring, MD, 20910. Send a SASE for free information. Phone hours 9A.M.–5P.M. EST.

Stepparenting

STEPFAMILY ASSOCIATION OF AMERICA—This association has groups that sponser self-help programs and education. They have 64 chapters and aid in starting up groups. They sell 50 different titles. Send a business-sized SASE, to 215 Centennial Mall South, Suite 212, Lincoln, Nebraska. A two-dollar donation is recommended. (402) 477-7837. Phone hours are Monday through Friday 8A.M.–4:30P.M. CST.

INDEX

About The Authors

John Alston is a native Californian. He graduated from Chapman College in Orange, received his masters in counseling psychology from California State University in Hayward. He has taught elementary, junior and senior high school, and served as a full time consultant to the Palo Alto Unified School District and coordinator of Curriculum and Staff Development in the Hayward Unified School District. Today he is in demand as a presenter of programs to both adults and youth throughout the United States and Canada. He lives in Los Angeles with his wife Karen and daughter Lindsay.

Brenda Lane Richardson is a journalist from Piedmont, California who has written for The New York Times and other publications. She was a 1982 Professional Journalism Fellow at Stanford University and winner of a 1985 Alicia Patterson Award.